Lazy Carnivore Diet Cookbook:

Improve Your Health, Boost Your Energy, and Shed Pounds with Hustle-Free, Quick, and Scrumptious Recipes with Pictures for Meat Lovers, Along with 90-Day Meal Plan

BY PHOEBE BUCKLEY

COPYRIGHT

Copyright © 2024 by Phoebe Buckley. All rights reserved. No part of this publication may be reproduced, distributed, or transmitted in any form or by any means, including photocopying, recording, or other electronic or mechanical methods, without the prior written permission of the author, except in the case of brief quotations embodied in critical reviews and specific other noncommercial uses permitted by copyright law.

Legal notice: This book, titled "Lazy Carnivore Diet Cookbook," is authored by Phoebe Buckley and is fully protected under copyright laws. Any unauthorized distribution, reproduction, or use of the book, in whole or part, is prohibited and may result in legal actions against you. Any use of this book without the author's or the publisher's permission violates their legal rights.

TABLE OF CONTENT

INTRODUCTION 1
CHAPTER 1: BASICS OF CARNIVORE DIET 2
How to get started 4
Transformative case studies 6
Fat-to-protein guides 7
Easy Clean-Up Hacks for Lazy Carnivores 10

CHAPTER 2 BREAKFAST 12

Beef & Egg Skillet	12	Veal Sweetbreads with Garlic Butter	16
Sausage & Egg Scramble	12	Carnivore Breakfast Pizza	16
Bacon & Egg Skillet	13	Smoked Pork Shoulder & Collagen Pancakes	17
Steak & Eggs	13	Bacon and Ricotta Egg Bake	17
Ground Beef & Cheese Scramble	14	Baked Egg and Gouda Cups	18
Carnivore Omelette	14	Ham and Mozzarella Breakfast Roll-Ups	18
Bacon & Ground Pork Scramble	15	Pork Sausage and Cream Cheese Omelette	19
Crispy Pork Belly Bites	15	Cheddar and Ham Breakfast Bake	19

CHAPTER 3 LUNCH 20

Pan-Seared Ribeye with Compound Butter	20	Smoked Salmon and Cream Cheese Roll-Ups	24
Lamb Meatballs with Bone Broth Gravy	20	Grilled Lamb Chops with Garlic Butter	24
Bison Stew with Bone Marrow	21	Baked Chicken Thighs with Mozzarella	25
Crispy Duck Breast	21	Bison Steaks with Bone Broth Reduction	25
Carnivore Shepherd's Pie	22	Pork Loin with Parmesan Crust	26
Pork Rind Crusted Chicken Thighs	22	Pork Chops with Crispy Skin	26
Beef Kidney and Bacon Stir-Fry	23	Grilled Beef Tongue with Mustard Sauce	27
Beef and Ricotta Stuffed Meatballs	23	Seared Venison Steaks with Herb Reduction	27

CHAPTER 4 DINNER 28

Creamy Chicken Thighs with Ricotta	28	Pan-Seared Rabbit with Thyme and Garlic	32
Pan-Seared Barramundi with Herb Butter	28	Pork Belly Skewers	32
Seared Beef Heart with Garlic Butter	29	Pork Tenderloin with Ghee	33
Grilled Pork Ribs with Bone Broth Glaze	29	Veal Cutlets with Ghee	33
Venison Steak with Mushroom Sauce	30	Bison Steak with Herb Butter	34
Baked Beef Short Ribs with Tallow	30	Carnivore Sushi Rolls	34
Lamb Shank with Fennel and Garlic	31	Stuffed Chicken Thighs with Bacon	35
Bison Meatballs with Bone Broth Gravy	31	Grilled Beef Kebabs with Bacon	35

CHAPTER 5 SOUPS AND STEWS 36

Chicken & Duck Fat Soup 36
Pork Belly and Beef Heart Stew 36
Carnivore Seafood Soup 37
Duck Breast and Beef Broth Soup 37
Lobster and Shrimp Stew 38

TABLE OF CONTENT

CHAPTER 6 SEAFOOD AND FISH...... 39

Lobster Tail with Garlic Butter...... 39
Grilled Shrimp with Lemon Butter...... 39
Tuna with Avocado...... 40
Grilled Swordfish with Herb Butter...... 40
Pan-Fried Salmon with Dill...... 41
Baked Cod with Olive Oil and Herbs...... 41
Grilled Octopus with Olive Oil...... 42
Scallop and Shrimp Stew...... 42
Grilled Mackerel with Garlic...... 43
Seared Scallops with Olive Oil...... 43
Grilled Calamari with Olive Oil...... 44
Grilled Sardines with Garlic and Herb Butter...... 44
Seared Halibut with Caper Butter Sauce...... 45
Grilled Prawns with Garlic and Lemon...... 45

CHAPTER 7 SNACKS...... 46

Pork Rind Nachos...... 46
Carnivore Meat Chips...... 46
Bacon-Wrapped Avocado Bites...... 47
Cheddar Cheese Chips...... 47
Deviled Eggs...... 48
Pepperoni Chips...... 48
Pork Cracklings...... 49
Bacon-Wrapped Scallops...... 49
Duck Fat Crisps...... 50
Turkey Bacon Bites...... 50

CHAPTER 8 SAUSES...... 51

Savory Beef Drippings Gravy...... 51
Bone Broth Béarnaise Sauce...... 51
Roasted Garlic and Tallow Sauce...... 52
Creamy Carnivore Garlic Butter Sauce...... 52

CHAPTER 9 DESSERTS...... 53

Carnivore Chocolate-Free Fudge...... 53
Carnivore Custard...... 53
Cheese Fat Bombs...... 54
Heavy Cream Panna Cotta...... 54
Carnivore Cheesecake Bites...... 55
Vanilla Butter Ice Cream...... 55

90-DAY MEAL PLAN...... 56

SHOPPING LIST...... 61

CONCLUSION...... 68

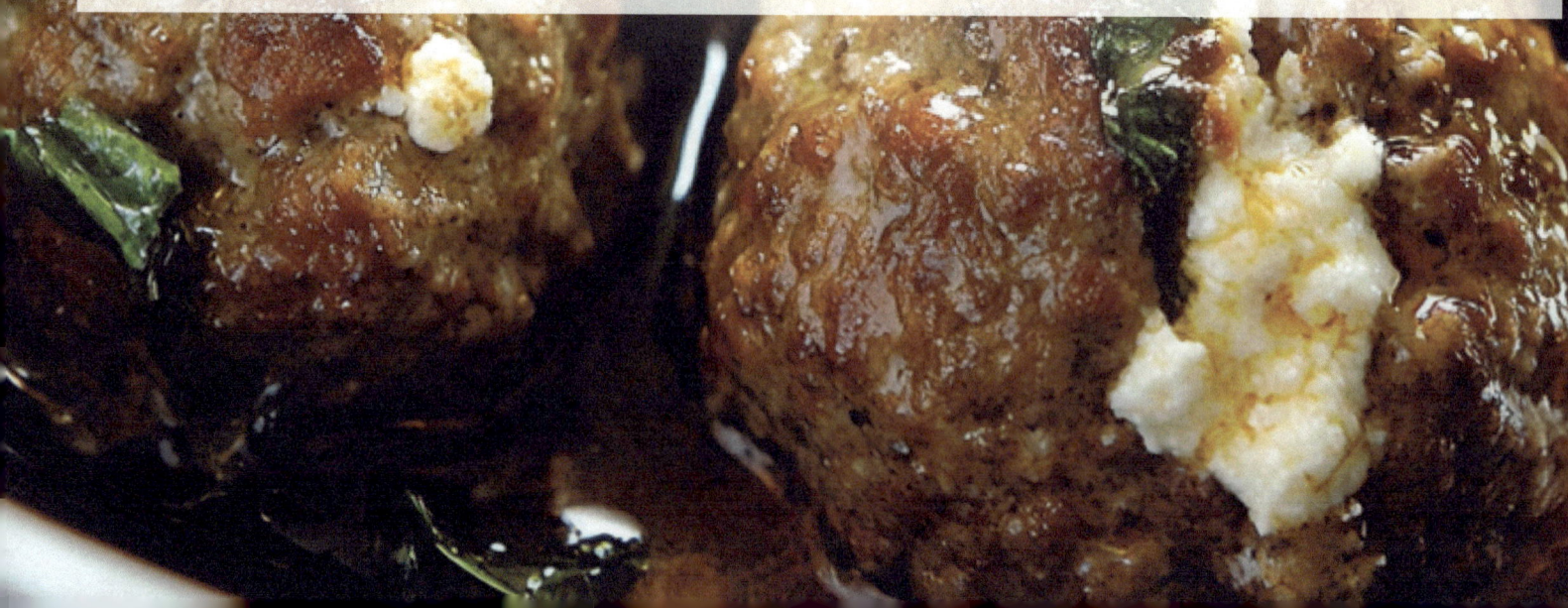

INTRODUCTION

The Lazy Carnivore Diet Cookbook is your gateway to a life-changing way of eating that's as simple as it is delicious. If you're tired of complicated diets and endless meal prep, this book is here to show you how effortless the carnivore lifestyle can be, without sacrificing flavor or variety.

I'm Phoebe Buckley, a nutritionist who discovered the life-changing power of the carnivore diet after battling obesity and health struggles for years. The results were incredible—weight loss, more energy, and feeling better than ever. Now, I'm here to share that journey with you in the easiest, most enjoyable way possible.

This cookbook is designed for people just like you—busy, on-the-go, and ready for a real change. The recipes are fast, easy, and packed with flavor. You'll find juicy steaks, crispy chicken, and tender roasts, all made with minimal ingredients and even less clean-up. And to make it even easier, the cookbook is filled with vibrant, mouthwatering pictures to guide you through—because who doesn't love cooking with a little visual inspiration?

But this book is more than just a collection of recipes. It's your personal roadmap to health. With a 90-day meal plan included, I'll guide you through step-by-step, so you never have to worry about what's for dinner. Whether you're looking to shed weight, improve your energy, or just feel your best, this meal plan is designed to help you hit your goals, one delicious meal at a time.

And let's talk about convenience. This cookbook is packed with one-pot recipes and grill-and-go meals that make cooking a breeze. Most recipes take minutes to prepare and are designed to be as easy on your schedule as they are on your taste buds. Imagine meals that are not only delicious but leave you with almost no clean-up! For anyone with a hectic lifestyle, this book is a game-changer.

If you're ready to experience a diet that's easy, satisfying, and life-changing, then let's dive in. This book is more than a guide—it's your ticket to a simpler, healthier way of life. Let's get started, and I promise you, this journey will be as delicious as it is transformational.

CHAPTER 1 BASICS OF CARNIVORE DIET

The carnivore diet isn't just another trend—it's a total game-changer for your health, energy, and even your mood. If you've ever dreamed of a diet that lets you eat steak for breakfast and still drop weight, you're in for a treat. The benefits go way beyond weight loss—this way of eating can transform your life in ways you never thought possible. Let's dive into why the carnivore diet is getting so much love!

BENEFITS OF CARNIVORE DIET

1. Effortless Weight Loss
Imagine eating ribeye, bacon, and juicy burgers while your body burns fat like a furnace. That's what happens on the carnivore diet. Because protein and fat keep you full for longer, you naturally eat less without feeling deprived or hungry. Your body becomes a fat-burning machine, and you don't even have to count calories or measure portions. People report dropping inches while feasting on some of the tastiest meals out there—what's not to love?

2. Endless Energy (Bye-Bye Afternoon Slumps)
Ever feel like you hit a wall around 2 p.m., needing coffee just to stay awake? On the carnivore diet, those afternoon slumps are history. Once your body switches to burning fat for fuel instead of carbs, you'll experience steady, lasting energy all day long. No more sugar crashes, no more mid-afternoon zombie mode—just smooth, consistent energy that keeps you focused and alert. Many carnivores say they haven't felt this energized since their teenage years!

3. Inflammation? Not Here
Kiss your aches and pains goodbye! Many plant foods contain compounds that can trigger inflammation in the body—think bloating, joint pain, or even skin issues. When you go carnivore, you eliminate those triggers. Whether it's arthritis, skin flare-ups, or just feeling stiff after a workout, the carnivore diet can calm that inflammation and get your body feeling smooth and pain-free again. Just ask the thousands of people who've said goodbye to their chronic pain after going meat-only!

4. Mental Clarity Like Never Before
Carnivores often talk about the incredible "mental clarity" they experience. Think of your brain running on premium fuel instead of the cheap stuff. With steady blood sugar and no more energy crashes, you'll find yourself thinking more clearly, concentrating better, and getting more done. Some people even report feeling like a fog has been lifted from their brain. Say goodbye to that sluggish, distracted feeling and hello to razor-sharp focus!

5. The Simplest Diet Ever
Let's be real: most diets are complicated, full of meal prep, ingredient hunting, and rules you have to memorize. The carnivore diet is the opposite. It's just meat. That's it! You don't need to worry about carbs, fiber, or fat grams—just cook up your favorite cut of meat, and you're good to go. Busy day? No problem—throw a steak on the grill or sear some burgers in a pan, and you've got dinner in minutes. Minimal prep, minimal clean-up, maximum flavor!

6. Gut Health, Simplified
Bloating, indigestion, and food intolerances are common issues for many people. But by removing plants and fiber—which can irritate your gut—the carnivore diet gives your digestive system a break. Carnivores often report feeling less bloated, and their digestion improves dramatically. In fact, some people with severe gut issues like IBS have found relief they never thought possible by going all-in on meat.

7. Balanced Hormones = Better Sleep, Mood, and Libido
Goodbye hormone rollercoasters! The carnivore diet supports your hormones in all the right ways. The healthy fats and proteins from animal foods help balance everything from your stress hormones to your sleep cycles, leading to better rest, improved mood, and yes, even a boost in your libido. It's like giving your body the fuel it's been craving to function at its best.

8. More Variety Than You'd Think
Steak and bacon are great, but don't think the carnivore diet stops there! With endless options—think lamb chops, pork belly, organ meats, and seafood—you'll never run out of delicious meals to try. Plus, the simplicity of the diet means you can focus on perfecting your favorite cuts and techniques without feeling overwhelmed by recipes.

9. Sustainable for Real Life
Unlike restrictive diets that you can only stick to for a few weeks, the carnivore diet is sustainable. You don't feel deprived, there's no complicated math, and the results—whether it's weight loss, more energy, or simply feeling amazing—motivate you to keep going. It's a lifestyle you can actually stick with long-term, and it doesn't feel like a constant battle.

In short, the carnivore diet is a life-saver for anyone who wants more energy, effortless fat loss, and simplified eating without all the noise of other diets. You'll not only feel and look better, but you'll also be feeding your body the nutrients it truly needs. Ready to experience the transformation for yourself? Dig in, the meat's waiting!

HOW TO GET STARTED

Getting started with the carnivore diet is exciting and surprisingly straightforward. This is a lifestyle where simplicity reigns, and the benefits can be life-changing. Let's explore how to jump into the carnivore way of eating and set yourself up for success with some easy, practical steps.

Keep It Simple, Satisfying, and Delicious
The core of the carnivore diet is blissfully simple: meat, animal fats, and water. That's it. No need for complicated recipes or long ingredient lists. Think juicy ribeye steaks, crispy bacon, tender roast chicken, or a perfectly grilled pork chop. Whether you're a seasoned chef or someone who barely steps into the kitchen, you can make satisfying, nutrient-rich meals with minimal effort.

Start by stocking up your kitchen with some carnivore essentials:
- **Beef**: Think ribeye, ground beef, brisket, or sirloin.
- **Pork**: Bacon, pork chops, pork belly, and sausages (just make sure they're without fillers).
- **Chicken**: Thighs, wings, drumsticks—anything with that perfect mix of fat and flavor.
- **Seafood**: Salmon, shrimp, mackerel, and sardines add variety and healthy fats.
- **Organ meats**: Liver, heart, and bone marrow, packed with nutrients.

Ease into It: Take Your Time to Adjust
Going full carnivore might feel like a big leap, especially if your diet has been full of carbs and plants. So, there's no harm in easing your way in. Start by cutting out processed foods, sugar, and grains, then gradually reduce fruits and vegetables as you feel ready. This gradual approach can help your body adjust without feeling overwhelmed.

Many people report that once they start eating primarily meat, their cravings for carbs and sugar naturally disappear. Your body begins to crave nutrient-dense food, and the shift becomes easier than expected.

Listen to Your Body: Eat When You're Hungry, Stop When You're Full
One of the best parts of the carnivore diet? No need to count calories or portion control! Just eat until you're satisfied. Protein and fat are incredibly filling, so you'll naturally eat less over time without even thinking about it. You'll notice that your hunger cues become clearer, and when you're full, you'll feel it without overeating. No guilt, no stress, just good food.

Hydration Is Key
As your body transitions from a carb-based diet to burning fat for fuel, it will shed excess water and sodium. It's important to stay hydrated during this time. Drink plenty of water, and don't be afraid to add a pinch of salt to your water or meals to help maintain your electrolyte balance.

If you experience symptoms like fatigue or headaches during the first week or two, don't panic. This is often referred to as the "keto flu"—a common phase while your body adjusts to its new energy source. These symptoms will pass, and your energy will come roaring back!

Variety Is the Spice of Carnivore Life
You might be thinking, "Won't I get bored of just eating meat?" The truth is, the carnivore diet offers far more variety than you'd expect. Think about the endless cuts of beef, pork, chicken, and seafood, not to mention the different ways to prepare them—grilling, slow-cooking, searing in a cast iron pan, or even experimenting with bone broth or jerky. And don't overlook organ meats, which are nutrient powerhouses and can add variety and depth to your meals.

Organ meats like liver are loaded with vitamins like A, B12, and iron—so you're getting a nutrient-dense meal in every bite!

Trust the Process: Results Will Come
As you dive into the carnivore lifestyle, give your body time to adjust. You might experience rapid benefits like reduced bloating, improved digestion, or clearer skin within a few days, but other changes like weight loss or energy boosts may take a bit longer. Be patient—your body is adjusting to a whole new way of fueling itself, and the results will follow.

Track Your Progress
While the diet itself is simple, it's helpful to track how you feel during the transition. Notice how your energy levels change, how your mental clarity sharpens, and how your body composition evolves. Taking note of these changes can keep you motivated, especially in those early days. Some people even like to take "before" photos or track their weight and measurements to see how their body transforms over time.

Connect with the Carnivore Community
Starting any new diet can feel like a solo mission, but it doesn't have to be. Connecting with the carnivore community—whether online or in person—can give you the support, motivation, and tips you need to succeed. The community is full of people who have been where you are, and they're eager to share advice, meal ideas, and encouragement.

Many carnivores share their transformation stories online, showing how much better they feel after switching to a meat-based diet. These real-life examples can be inspiring as you begin your own journey.

TRANSFORMATIVE CASE STUDIES

The carnivore diet is a powerful lifestyle that has completely transformed the health, energy, and lives of countless people around the world. From weight loss to autoimmune recovery, these case studies highlight how going all-in on meat has led to life-changing results. Let's dive into some real-world examples of people who've experienced remarkable transformations on the carnivore diet.

Sarah – From Chronic Fatigue to Supercharged Energy

Sarah was a busy mom of three who had been battling chronic fatigue for years. No matter what she tried—different diets, exercise routines, or sleep aids—nothing seemed to give her the energy she needed to get through the day. After hearing about the carnivore diet, Sarah decided to give it a try, hoping to get rid of the daily brain fog and exhaustion.

The Result? Within a few weeks of switching to the carnivore diet, Sarah experienced a surge in energy she hadn't felt in years. Without carbs weighing her down, her body began running on fat for fuel, giving her long-lasting, stable energy. Not only did she ditch the afternoon naps, but she also started waking up refreshed and ready to tackle her day. As a bonus, she lost 20 pounds over the first two months without even trying.

David – Reversing Autoimmune Symptoms

David had been living with rheumatoid arthritis for over a decade. His daily routine was shaped by joint pain, inflammation, and stiffness, forcing him to rely on medications just to manage the pain. But the side effects of the medications were becoming unbearable, and David knew he needed a different solution. After researching the anti-inflammatory benefits of the carnivore diet, he decided to give it a shot.

The Result? After transitioning to a carnivore diet, David's joint pain significantly reduced within just a month. He was able to wean himself off medications as the inflammation in his body decreased. Six months in, he was virtually pain-free, with full mobility in his joints. His rheumatoid arthritis symptoms, once debilitating, were now under control, all thanks to his commitment to a meat-only lifestyle. For David, the carnivore diet didn't just help with his weight—it gave him back his quality of life.

Jake – From Pre-Diabetic to Healthy Blood Sugar Levels

At 45, Jake was diagnosed as pre-diabetic, with his doctor warning that he was on the fast track to full-blown diabetes if he didn't make a serious change. With high blood sugar levels and a family history of diabetes, Jake knew he had to act quickly. After reading about the carnivore diet's ability to stabilize blood sugar, he decided to give it a try.

The Result? Within weeks of adopting the carnivore diet, Jake's blood sugar levels normalized. He continued the diet for six months, and at his next doctor's appointment, his pre-diabetic diagnosis was completely reversed. His fasting glucose levels were back in the healthy range, and his doctor was shocked by how quickly the diet had transformed his health. Jake also dropped 25 pounds during the process and felt stronger and more energetic than he had in years. The carnivore diet didn't just help him avoid diabetes—it gave him a new lease on life.

Mike – Building Muscle and Boosting Athletic Performance

Mike was an avid gym-goer and amateur bodybuilder, but he hit a plateau in both his muscle gains and his overall performance. Despite sticking to a traditional high-carb, high-protein diet, his progress had stalled. After hearing that the carnivore diet could optimize muscle recovery and athletic performance, Mike made the switch.

The Result? Within a few months on the carnivore diet, Mike noticed faster recovery times, improved strength, and better muscle definition. His workouts felt more explosive, and he no longer experienced the same level of soreness after training. The nutrient density of the diet, combined with its high-fat, high-protein focus, helped Mike break through his plateau and take his fitness to the next level. He was amazed by how well his body responded to an all-meat diet, even in an intense athletic environment.

These transformative stories show that the carnivore diet is more than just another eating plan—it has the power to radically improve health, energy, and well-being across the board. Whether you're dealing with chronic health issues, struggling with weight, or simply looking to feel your best, the carnivore diet has helped people from all walks of life achieve incredible, lasting results.

FAT-TO-PROTEIN RATIO GUIDES

One of the key components to thriving on the carnivore diet is understanding how to balance your fat-to-protein ratio. Getting this ratio right can have a big impact on how you feel, your energy levels, and whether you hit your specific health goals, whether it's weight loss, muscle gain, or simply improving your overall well-being. Let's dive into why this balance matters and how you can tailor it to fit your needs.

Why Does Fat-to-Protein Ratio Matter?

Protein and fat are the two cornerstones of the carnivore diet, but how much of each you consume can influence everything from weight loss and satiety to energy levels and mental clarity. While protein helps build and repair muscle, and keeps you full, fat is your primary energy source on the carnivore diet. The right ratio between these two macronutrients can make all the difference in how you feel and perform day to day.

General Fat-to-Protein Guidelines

For weight loss: Higher fat, moderate protein.
For muscle gain: Higher protein, moderate fat.
For overall health and maintenance: Balanced fat and protein.

But this isn't a one-size-fits-all approach. Everyone's body is different, so adjusting the ratio based on how you feel and your goals is key.

Fat-to-protein Ratios for Different Goals:

Weight Loss: Prioritize Fat for Satiety and Energy

When your goal is to lose weight, you'll want to keep fat intake higher than protein. This helps you stay in a at-burning state while keeping your body satisfied with fewer cravings and hunger pangs. A higher fat intake also provides steady energy, making it easier to sustain the diet long-term.
Suggested ratio: 70% fat to 30% protein.
Example foods: Ribeye steak, pork belly, fatty ground beef, butter, and tallow.

By keeping fat intake high, your body will efficiently burn stored fat for energy, promoting weight loss while keeping you feeling full and satisfied after meals. The key is not to fear fat—embrace it as your main source of fuel!

Muscle Gain: Focus on Protein for Growth and Recovery

If building muscle is your priority, you'll want to increase your protein intake to ensure your body has what it needs for muscle repair and growth. Fat is still important for energy, but a slightly higher protein ratio helps promote muscle recovery and strength gains.
Suggested ratio: 60% protein to 40% fat.
Example foods: Lean cuts of steak (sirloin, flank steak), chicken breast, turkey, eggs, and fish like tuna and cod.

This higher protein intake helps fuel intense workouts and gives your muscles the building blocks they need to grow. By pairing moderate fat with high protein, you can still maintain your energy without feeling sluggish.

For Overall Health and Maintenance: Balanced Approach

If your goal is simply to maintain your current weight and improve general health, you'll want a more balanced ratio of fat and protein. This ensures your body gets enough fat for energy while getting sufficient protein for muscle preservation and repair.
Suggested ratio: 50% fat to 50% protein.
Example foods: Equal portions of fattier cuts like ribeye or pork shoulder along with leaner options like chicken thighs or ground beef.

This balance works well for those who are happy with their weight and muscle mass but want to focus on long-term health. It's flexible and provides the best of both worlds—plenty of energy from fat and enough protein to maintain muscle.

Adjusting Your Fat-to-Protein Ratio

One of the great things about the carnivore diet is its flexibility. You can experiment with different fat-to-protein ratios to see what works best for your body. Pay attention to how you feel. Are you getting enough energy? Do you feel full after meals? Is your digestion improving? These are all signs that you've found the right balance.

Here's how to tweak your ratio:

-If you're feeling sluggish or lacking energy, increase your fat intake. Fat is your body's fuel on the carnivore diet, so more fat can help you feel more energized.
- If you're struggling with cravings, try increasing your fat intake, which can help with satiety and prevent overeating.
- If you're not seeing muscle growth, slightly increase your protein intake to support muscle recovery. Keep track of how your body responds and adjust your ratios as needed.

How to Measure Your Fat-to-Protein Ratio

Measuring your fat-to-protein ratio doesn't need to be overly complicated. You can start by focusing on choosing the right cuts of meat:
- High-fat cuts: Ribeye, pork belly, lamb chops, ground beef (80/20).
- Moderate-fat cuts: Chicken thighs, salmon, ground beef (90/10).
- Low-fat cuts: Sirloin, chicken breast, cod.

Additionally, you can add fats like butter, ghee, tallow, or cream to your meals to boost your fat intake.
For example, if you're eating a leaner cut like chicken breast or sirloin, add some butter or tallow for cooking. This helps balance the protein with fat for energy, especially if you're aiming for weight loss or higher energy levels.

Listening to Your Body

Ultimately, the best fat-to-protein ratio is the one that makes you feel your best. As you go along, listen to your body's signals. If you're satisfied, energized, and seeing results, you're likely on the right track. The flexibility of the carnivore diet allows you to experiment and adjust until you find the sweet spot that helps you reach your goals, whether it's weight loss, muscle gain, or overall health.

By understanding and mastering the balance between fat and protein, you can tailor your carnivore diet to meet your unique needs, unlocking the full potential of this powerful way of eating.

EASY CLEAN-UP HACKS FOR LAZY CARNIVORES

Let's be honest—no one loves the clean-up that comes after a delicious meal. But if you're embracing the carnivore diet, the good news is that your kitchen can stay as clean and simple as your plate. With a few clever tricks, you can enjoy your juicy steaks, crispy bacon, and tender ribs without turning your kitchen into a greasy battlefield. Here's how you can cook like a carnivore with barely any clean-up, so you can get back to what really matters—eating that perfect ribeye!

Embrace One-Pot and One-Pan Meals

Who doesn't love a meal that only dirties one pot? Whether you're grilling, roasting, or frying up your favorite cut of meat, a one-pan or one-pot meal is your best friend. You can sear your meat, pop it in the oven, and let it cook to perfection—all in the same cast iron skillet or sheet pan. Not only does this save you from juggling a bunch of dirty dishes, but it also keeps your kitchen chaos-free.

Pro Tip: Cook your steak in a cast iron skillet, then throw it in the oven to finish. One dish, zero stress, maximum flavor.

The Magic of Foil and Parchment Paper

Want a clean sheet pan without the scrub? Line your pans with foil or parchment paper before cooking, and boom—instant clean-up hack. The meat juices and fat stay on the liner, so you can just toss it when you're done, leaving your pan spotless. This trick works wonders when roasting bacon or fatty cuts like pork belly, saving you from scrubbing off layers of baked-on grease.

Pro Tip: Crumple the foil slightly before lining your pan. It helps elevate your meat so it doesn't sit in grease, giving you that perfect crispy finish while keeping the mess to a minimum!

Let the Slow Cooker or Air Fryer Do the Heavy Lifting

Why not let your appliances do the hard work and keep things clean? Air fryers and slow cookers are kitchen saviors when it comes to easy clean-up. Throw your meat in, let the machine do the cooking, and when you're done, all you have to wash is one basket or pot. Bonus points if you use a slow cooker liner—just toss it, and you've basically got zero clean-up to worry about.

Pro Tip: Air fryers are especially great for crispy carnivore snacks like bacon or chicken wings—just one basket to clean, and you get perfectly cooked food every time.

Cook in Bulk, Clean Once

Why clean up multiple times when you can do it all in one go? Batch cooking is a carnivore's dream—roast or grill a week's worth of meat all at once, and you've got minimal clean-up to deal with for days. Simply cook large portions, divide them into containers, and you'll be set for easy meals without having to scrub pans every night.

Pro Tip: Use one sheet pan to cook a variety of meats—throw some sausages, chicken thighs, and a couple of steaks on one tray, and you've got a carnivore feast with just one pan to clean.

The Grill is Your Friend

Not only does grilling give you that smoky, charred flavor we all love, but it also keeps the mess outdoors. Forget scrubbing pans or cleaning stovetops—just fire up the grill, cook your meat to perfection, and when you're done, a quick brush down is all you need. Even better? No greasy stovetop splatter to clean up.

Pro Tip: If you're not in the mood to grill outdoors, a stovetop grill pan can give you the same effect with minimal mess—just toss it in the dishwasher after a quick scrub.

Wipe As You Go

This trick may sound simple, but it's a game-changer. Keep a damp cloth or paper towel nearby while you cook, and wipe down surfaces as soon as fat splatters or juices drip. By doing this while cooking, you avoid grease hardening into a sticky mess. No one likes scrubbing dried-on fat, so wipe it up while it's fresh and save yourself from a bigger headache later.

Pro Tip: For stubborn grease spots, keep some vinegar or a degreaser nearby—it makes wiping down surfaces even easier.

Let the Oven Do the Work

Roasting your meat in the oven not only gives you delicious, even cooking, but it also contains all the mess in one pan. Oven-roasting means no grease splattering all over your stovetop, and if you line your tray with foil or parchment, the clean-up is a breeze. Let the oven handle the hard work while you kick back.

Pro Tip: Place a wire rack over your pan so the meat doesn't sit in its own fat. It'll get nice and crispy, and the clean-up will be even easier since the juices drip away from the meat.

Invest in Reusable Cooking Accessories

Reusable silicone baking mats are your new best friends when it comes to cooking on sheet pans. These non-stick mats keep fat and meat juices from sticking to your trays, making clean-up a breeze. Just give the mat a quick rinse (or pop it in the dishwasher), and you're done! Plus, they're environmentally friendly—no more tossing parchment paper after every roast.

Pro Tip: Use a silicone mat to roast pork rinds, bake carnivore snacks, or even cook greasy cuts like duck—all without worrying about stuck-on fat.

Pre-Cut and Portion Your Meat

Cutting up large pieces of meat can leave you with a messy cutting board and counter. But if you pre-cut and portion your meats as soon as you bring them home, you'll only have to deal with the mess once. After that, it's grab-and-cook simplicity. Plus, it makes weeknight meals much faster when you've already done the prep work ahead of time.

Pro Tip: Keep a dedicated cutting board for raw meat to make clean-up even easier and prevent any cross-contamination.

Hot Water is Your Secret Weapon

After you're done cooking, hit those pans with hot water immediately. The heat melts away fat and grease before it has a chance to harden, making scrubbing a thing of the past. Even if you don't feel like washing dishes right away, a quick rinse with hot water can save you from the dreaded baked-on grease later.

Pro Tip: For especially stubborn grease, sprinkle a little baking soda into the hot water and let it sit for a few minutes. It'll break down the fat and make clean-up a breeze.

With these easy clean-up hacks, you'll spend less time scrubbing and more time enjoying the mouthwatering meals you've cooked up. Whether it's lining your pans with foil, using the grill, or embracing one-pot wonders, keeping your kitchen clean is easier than ever. Now go ahead, feast like a carnivore—without the mess!

CHAPTER 2 BREAKFAST
BEEF & EGG SKILLET

Prep Time: 5 minutes | Cook Time: 15 minutes | Total Time: 20 minutes | Yield: 4 servings
Nutritional Breakdown (Estimated per serving): Calories: 450 kcal, Protein: 30 g, Fat: 35 g, Carbs: 0 g

Ingredients:
- 1 lb ground beef (80/20)
- 6 large eggs
- 1 tbsp butter
- Salt and pepper to taste

Instructions:
1. Cook Beef: Heat a large skillet over medium heat and melt the butter. Add the ground beef, breaking it apart with a spatula. Cook for 10 minutes, stirring occasionally, until browned and fully cooked.
2. Cook Eggs: Push the beef to one side of the skillet. Crack eggs into the empty space and cook over medium heat. Scramble the eggs or cook them sunny-side up as preferred. This will take 3-5 minutes.
3. Serve: Mix the cooked eggs with the beef, season with salt and pepper, and serve immediately.

SAUSAGE & EGG SCRAMBLE

Prep Time: 5 minutes | Cook Time: 15 minutes | Total Time: 20 minutes | Yield: 4 servings
Nutritional Breakdown (Estimated per serving): Calories: 450 kcal, Protein: 25 g, Fat: 35 g, Carbs: 0 g

Ingredients:
- 4 pork sausages
- 6 large eggs
- 1 tbsp butter
- Salt and pepper to taste

Instructions:
1. Cook Sausages: Heat a skillet over medium heat and add the butter. Once melted, add the sausages and cook for 8-10 minutes, turning occasionally, until browned and fully cooked. Remove from heat and slice into rounds.
2. Cook Eggs: In the same skillet, crack the eggs directly into the pan and scramble them with the sausage slices. Cook for about 5 minutes, stirring occasionally until the eggs are set.
3. Serve: Season with salt and pepper to taste and serve hot.

BACON & EGG SKILLET

Prep Time: 5 minutes | Cook Time: 10 minutes | Total Time: 15 minutes | Yield: 4 servings
Nutritional Breakdown (Estimated per serving): Calories: 400 kcal, Protein: 25 g, Fat: 35 g, Carbs: 0 g

Ingredients:
- 12 slices thick-cut bacon
- 8 large eggs
- Salt and pepper to taste

Instructions:
1. Cook Bacon: Heat a large skillet over medium heat. Add bacon slices and cook for about 5-7 minutes, turning halfway, until crispy. Remove bacon and set aside on a paper towel to drain.
2. Cook Eggs: In the same skillet, using the rendered bacon grease, crack the eggs into the pan. Cook sunny-side up for 3-4 minutes or scramble them if preferred.
3. Serve: Arrange the crispy bacon on top of the eggs and season with salt and pepper to taste.

STEAK & EGGS

Prep Time: 5 minutes | Cook Time: 15 minutes | Total Time: 20 minutes | Yield: 2 servings
Nutritional Breakdown (Estimated per serving): Calories: 550 kcal, Protein: 40 g, Fat: 45 g, Carbs: 0 g

Ingredients:
- 2 ribeye steaks
- 4 large eggs
- 1 tbsp butter
- Salt and pepper to taste

Instructions:
1. Cook Steak: Heat butter in a skillet over medium-high heat. Season the ribeye steaks with salt and pepper. Sear the steaks for 4-5 minutes per side for medium-rare (adjust cooking time for preferred doneness).
2. Rest Steaks: Remove the steaks from the skillet and let them rest for 5 minutes.
3. Cook Eggs: In the same skillet, crack the eggs and cook over medium heat to your desired doneness, about 2-4 minutes.
4. Serve: Serve the steaks with the eggs on the side and season with additional salt and pepper if needed.

GROUND BEEF & CHEESE SCRAMBLE

Prep Time: 5 minutes | Cook Time: 15 minutes | Total Time: 20 minutes | Yield: 4 servings
Nutritional Breakdown (Estimated per serving): Calories: 500 kcal, Protein: 30 g, Fat: 40 g, Carbs: 0 g

Ingredients:
- 1 lb ground beef
- 1 cup shredded cheddar cheese
- 6 large eggs
- 1 tbsp butter

Instructions:
1. Cook Ground Beef: Heat butter in a large skillet over medium heat. Add the ground beef and cook for about 8 minutes, breaking it apart with a spatula until browned and fully cooked.
2. Cook Eggs: Add eggs to the beef and scramble for 3-4 minutes until the eggs are fully set.
3. Add Cheese: Sprinkle shredded cheddar cheese on top and stir for 1-2 minutes until melted.
4. Serve: Serve hot.

CARNIVORE OMELETTE

Prep Time: 5 minutes | Cook Time: 10 minutes | Total Time: 15 minutes | Yield: 2 servings
Nutritional Breakdown (Estimated per serving): Calories: 500 kcal, Protein: 30 g, Fat: 45 g, Carbs: 0 g

Ingredients:
- 4 large eggs
- 1 cup shredded cheddar cheese
- 1/2 cup cooked ground beef
- 1 tbsp butter
- Salt and pepper to taste

Instructions:
1. Cook Omelette: Heat butter in a skillet over medium heat. Whisk the eggs in a bowl and pour them into the skillet. Let cook for 3-4 minutes until the eggs are mostly set.
2. Add Fillings: Add cooked ground beef and cheese to one side of the omelette. Fold the omelette over the fillings and cook for an additional 2-3 minutes until the cheese is melted.
3. Serve: Season with salt and pepper and serve.

BACON & GROUND PORK SCRAMBLE

Prep Time: 5 minutes | Cook Time: 15 minutes | Total Time: 20 minutes | Yield: 4 servings
Nutritional Breakdown (Estimated per serving): Calories: 450 kcal, Protein: 30 g, Fat: 40 g, Carbs: 0 g

Ingredients:
- 6 slices bacon, chopped
- 1 lb ground pork
- 6 large eggs
- Salt and pepper to taste

Instructions:
1. Cook Bacon: Heat a skillet over medium heat. Add the chopped bacon and cook for about 5 minutes until crispy.
2. Cook Ground Pork: Add the ground pork to the skillet with the bacon and cook for 8-10 minutes, stirring occasionally until browned.
3. Cook Eggs: Crack the eggs into the skillet and scramble with the pork and bacon. Cook for 3-4 minutes until the eggs are fully cooked.
4. Serve: Season with salt and pepper and serve.

CRISPY PORK BELLY BITES

Prep Time: 5 minutes | Cook Time: 20 minutes | Total Time: 25 minutes | Yield: 4 servings
Nutritional Breakdown (Estimated per serving): Calories: 600 kcal, Protein: 35 g, Fat: 55 g, Carbs: 0 g

Ingredients:
- 1 lb pork belly, cubed
- Salt to taste

Instructions:
1. Cook Pork Belly: Heat a large skillet over medium-high heat. Add the pork belly cubes in a single layer. Cook for 15-20 minutes, stirring occasionally, until the cubes are crispy and golden brown on all sides.
2. Serve: Remove the pork belly from the skillet and sprinkle with salt. Serve crispy pork belly bites hot.

VEAL SWEETBREADS WITH GARLIC BUTTER

Prep Time: 10 minutes | Cook Time: 15 minutes | Total Time: 25 minutes | Yield: 4 servings
Nutritional Breakdown (Estimated per serving): Calories: 500 kcal, Protein: 35 g, Fat: 40 g, Carbs: 0 g

Ingredients:
- 1 lb veal sweetbreads, rinsed and patted dry
- 2 tbsp butter
- 2 cloves garlic, minced
- Salt and pepper to taste

Instructions:
1. Cook Sweetbreads: Heat butter in a skillet over medium-high heat. Add the sweetbreads and cook for 6-8 minutes, turning occasionally, until browned on all sides.
2. Add Garlic: Lower the heat to medium, add minced garlic, and cook for an additional 5 minutes, stirring to coat the sweetbreads with the garlic butter.
3. Serve: Season with salt and pepper and serve hot.

CARNIVORE BREAKFAST PIZZA

Prep Time: 5 minutes | Cook Time: 20 minutes | Total Time: 25 minutes | Yield: 4 servings
Nutritional Breakdown (Estimated per serving): Calories: 700 kcal, Protein: 50 g, Fat: 60 g, Carbs: 0 g

Ingredients:
- 1 lb ground beef
- 1/2 lb ground pork
- 1 cup shredded mozzarella cheese
- 1/2 cup heavy cream
- 2 tbsp butter

Instructions:
1. Cook Meat Base: In a large skillet, heat the butter over medium heat. Add the ground beef and pork and cook for about 10 minutes, breaking the meat apart until fully browned.
2. Add Cheese & Cream: Lower the heat to medium-low. Pour in the heavy cream and sprinkle the shredded mozzarella on top. Cook for 5-7 minutes, until the cheese melts and forms a "pizza" layer on top of the meat.
3. Serve: Cut the "pizza" into slices and serve.

SMOKED PORK SHOULDER & COLLAGEN PANCAKES

Prep Time: 10 minutes | **Cook Time:** 15 minutes | **Total Time:** 25 minutes | **Yield:** 4 servings
Nutritional Breakdown (Estimated per serving): Calories: 650 kcal, Protein: 45 g, Fat: 55 g, Carbs: 0 g

Ingredients:
- 1 lb smoked pork shoulder, shredded
- 1/2 cup collagen powder
- 1/2 cup heavy cream
- 2 tbsp butter

Instructions:
1. Prepare Pancake Batter: In a mixing bowl, combine collagen powder and heavy cream to create a thick batter.
2. Cook Pancakes: Heat butter in a skillet over medium heat. Scoop the collagen batter into the skillet, forming small pancakes. Cook for 2-3 minutes on each side until golden brown.
3. Serve: Top each pancake with a portion of the shredded smoked pork shoulder and serve hot.

BACON AND RICOTTA EGG BAKE

Prep Time: 5 minutes | **Cook Time:** 20 minutes | **Total Time:** 25 minutes | **Yield:** 4 servings
Nutritional Breakdown (Estimated per serving): Calories: 500 kcal, Protein: 35 g, Fat: 40 g, Carbs: 1 g

Ingredients:
- 6 slices bacon, chopped
- 6 eggs
- 1/2 cup ricotta cheese
- Salt and pepper to taste

Instructions:
1. Cook Bacon: Preheat oven to 375°F. Cook bacon in a skillet over medium heat until crispy, about 5-7 minutes.
2. Mix Eggs: In a bowl, whisk eggs, stir in ricotta, and add the cooked bacon. Season with salt and pepper.
3. Bake: Pour mixture into a greased dish and bake for 15-20 minutes, or until set.
4. Serve: Let it rest for a minute before serving warm.

BAKED EGG AND GOUDA CUPS

Prep Time: 5 minutes | **Cook Time:** 15 minutes | **Total Time:** 20 minutes | **Yield:** 2 servings
Nutritional Breakdown (Estimated per serving): Calories: 400 kcal, Protein: 30 g, Fat: 35 g, Carbs: 1 g

Ingredients:
- 4 eggs
- 1/4 cup shredded gouda cheese
- Salt to taste

Instructions:
1. Prep Eggs: Preheat oven to 375°F. Crack eggs into greased muffin tin cups.
2. Add Cheese: Sprinkle gouda cheese over each egg.
3. Bake: Bake for 12-15 minutes, until eggs are set and cheese melts.
4. Serve: Serve warm with salt to taste.

HAM AND MOZZARELLA BREAKFAST ROLL-UPS

Prep Time: 5 minutes | **Cook Time:** 10 minutes | **Total Time:** 15 minutes | **Yield:** 2 servings
Nutritional Breakdown (Estimated per serving): Calories: 450 kcal, Protein: 30 g, Fat: 35 g, Carbs: 1 g

Ingredients:
- 4 slices ham
- 4 eggs
- 1/4 cup shredded mozzarella cheese
- Salt to taste

Instructions:
1. Scramble Eggs: Scramble eggs in a skillet over medium heat for 5-6 minutes until cooked.
2. Assemble: Place scrambled eggs on ham slices, sprinkle with cheese, and roll them up.
3. Heat Roll-Ups: Warm the roll-ups in the skillet for 2-3 minutes until cheese melts.
4. Serve: Serve hot.

PORK SAUSAGE AND CREAM CHEESE OMELETTE

Prep Time: 5 minutes | **Cook Time:** 10 minutes | **Total Time:** 15 minutes | **Yield:** 2 servings
Nutritional Breakdown (Estimated per serving): Calories: 500 kcal, Protein: 35 g, Fat: 40 g, Carbs: 1 g

Ingredients:
- 4 eggs
- 1/2 lb pork sausage, crumbled
- 2 tbsp cream cheese
- 1 tbsp butter
- Salt to taste

Instructions:
1. Cook Sausage: Heat a skillet over medium heat. Add crumbled pork sausage and cook for 6-7 minutes until browned.
2. Cook Omelette: Whisk eggs and pour them into the skillet over the sausage. Cook until partially set, about 3 minutes.
3. Add Cream Cheese: Add cream cheese in small dollops, fold the omelette, and cook for another 2 minutes until fully set.
4. Serve: Serve warm and season with salt.

CHEDDAR AND HAM BREAKFAST BAKE

Prep Time: 5 minutes | **Cook Time:** 20 minutes | **Total Time:** 25 minutes | **Yield:** 4 servings
Nutritional Breakdown (Estimated per serving): Calories: 600 kcal, Protein: 40 g, Fat: 50 g, Carbs: 2 g

Ingredients:
- 6 eggs
- 1/2 cup diced ham
- 1/2 cup shredded cheddar cheese
- Salt to taste

Instructions:
1. Prepare Bake: Preheat oven to 375°F. In a greased baking dish, whisk eggs, stir in diced ham and cheddar cheese.
2. Bake: Bake for 18-20 minutes, or until the eggs are fully set and golden on top.
3. Serve: Let cool for 2 minutes before slicing and serving warm.

CHAPTER 3 LUNCH

PAN-SEARED RIBEYE WITH COMPOUND BUTTER

Prep Time: 5 minutes | **Cook Time:** 10 minutes | **Total Time:** 15 minutes | **Yield:** 2 servings
Nutritional Breakdown (Estimated per serving): Calories: 900 kcal, Protein: 60 g, Fat: 75 g, Carbs: 0 g

Ingredients:
- 2 ribeye steaks
- 4 tbsp butter (softened)
- 1 tsp minced garlic
- Salt and pepper to taste

Instructions:
1. Cook Ribeyes: Heat a skillet over high heat. Sear ribeye steaks for 4-5 minutes per side until they reach your preferred doneness.
2. Make Compound Butter: While the steaks are cooking, mix softened butter with minced garlic.
3. Serve: Once the steaks are done, top them with the garlic butter and serve hot.

LAMB MEATBALLS WITH BONE BROTH GRAVY

Prep Time: 10 minutes | **Cook Time:** 20 minutes | **Total Time:** 30 minutes | **Yield:** 4 servings
Nutritional Breakdown (Estimated per serving): Calories: 600 kcal, Protein: 40 g, Fat: 50 g, Carbs: 0 g

Ingredients:
- 1 lb ground lamb
- 1/2 cup crushed pork rinds
- 1 cup bone broth
- 1 tbsp butter

Instructions:
1. Form Meatballs: In a bowl, mix the ground lamb and crushed pork rinds. Form the mixture into meatballs.
2. Cook Meatballs: Heat butter in a skillet over medium heat. Add the meatballs and cook for about 15 minutes, turning occasionally, until browned and cooked through.
3. Make Gravy: Pour bone broth into the skillet and simmer for 5 minutes until the broth thickens into a gravy.
4. Serve: Serve the meatballs with the bone broth gravy on top.

BISON STEW WITH BONE MARROW

Prep Time: 10 minutes | **Cook Time:** 20 minutes | **Total Time:** 30 minutes | **Yield:** 4 servings
Nutritional Breakdown (Estimated per serving): Calories: 700 kcal, Protein: 50 g, Fat: 60 g, Carbs: 0 g

Ingredients:
- 1 lb bison stew meat
- 4 beef marrow bones
- 2 tbsp tallow
- Salt to taste

Instructions:
1. Cook Bison: Heat tallow in a large skillet over medium heat. Add bison stew meat and brown for about 10 minutes, stirring occasionally until browned.
2. Add Marrow Bones: Add the marrow bones to the skillet, cover, and cook for another 10 minutes until the marrow is soft and the bison is tender.
3. Serve: Scoop out the marrow and mix it with the bison stew meat. Season with salt and serve hot.

CRISPY DUCK BREAST

Prep Time: 5 minutes | **Cook Time:** 15 minutes | **Total Time:** 20 minutes | **Yield:** 2 servings
Nutritional Breakdown (Estimated per serving): Calories: 600 kcal, Protein: 40 g, Fat: 50 g, Carbs: 0 g

Ingredients:
- 2 duck breasts, skin-on
- Salt to taste

Instructions:
1. Cook Duck: Heat a skillet over medium heat. Place the duck breasts skin-side down and cook for 8-10 minutes until the skin is crispy. Flip the duck and cook for another 5 minutes until the meat reaches your preferred doneness.
2. Serve: Remove from heat, season with salt, and serve hot.

CARNIVORE SHEPHERD'S PIE

Prep Time: 10 minutes | Cook Time: 20 minutes | Total Time: 30 minutes | Yield: 4 servings
Nutritional Breakdown (Estimated per serving): Calories: 600 kcal, Protein: 40 g, Fat: 50 g, Carbs: 0 g

Ingredients:
- 1 lb ground beef
- 1/2 lb ground lamb
- 1 cup bone broth
- Salt to taste

Instructions:
1. Cook Meat: Heat a large skillet over medium heat. Add ground beef and ground lamb, cooking for about 10 minutes until fully browned and cooked through.
2. Add Broth: Pour in the bone broth and simmer for another 10 minutes, allowing the broth to reduce slightly.
3. Serve: Scoop the meat mixture into individual serving dishes or bowls and enjoy as a carnivore-friendly shepherd's pie.

PORK RIND CRUSTED CHICKEN THIGHS

Prep Time: 5 minutes | Cook Time: 20 minutes | Total Time: 25 minutes | Yield: 4 servings
Nutritional Breakdown (Estimated per serving): Calories: 600 kcal, Protein: 40 g, Fat: 50 g, Carbs: 0 g

Ingredients:
- 4 chicken thighs
- 1/2 cup crushed pork rinds
- Salt to taste

Instructions:
1. Coat Chicken Thighs: Press the chicken thighs firmly into the crushed pork rinds, ensuring they are evenly coated.
2. Cook Chicken: Heat a skillet over medium-high heat. Add the chicken thighs and cook for 15-20 minutes, flipping halfway through, until crispy and fully cooked.
3. Serve: Season with salt and serve hot.

BEEF KIDNEY AND BACON STIR-FRY

Prep Time: 5 minutes | Cook Time: 15 minutes | Total Time: 20 minutes | Yield: 4 servings
Nutritional Breakdown (Estimated per serving): Calories: 450 kcal, Protein: 35 g, Fat: 35 g, Carbs: 0 g

Ingredients:
- 1/2 lb beef kidney, diced
- 6 slices bacon, chopped
- 1 tbsp tallow
- Salt to taste

Instructions:
1. Cook Bacon: Heat a skillet over medium heat. Add the chopped bacon and cook for 5-7 minutes until crispy.
2. Cook Kidney: Add the tallow and diced beef kidney to the skillet, cooking for 8-10 minutes until browned and fully cooked.
3. Serve: Season with salt and serve hot.

BEEF AND RICOTTA STUFFED MEATBALLS

Prep Time: 10 minutes | Cook Time: 15 minutes | Total Time: 25 minutes | Yield: 4 servings
Nutritional Breakdown (Estimated per serving): Calories: 600 kcal, Protein: 45 g, Fat: 50 g, Carbs: 1 g

Ingredients:
- 1 lb ground beef
- 1/2 cup ricotta cheese
- Salt to taste

Instructions:
1. Prepare Meatballs: Form ground beef into meatballs, stuffing each with 1 tsp of ricotta cheese.
2. Cook Meatballs: Heat a skillet over medium heat and cook the meatballs for 12-15 minutes, turning occasionally until browned and cooked through.
3. Serve: Season with salt and serve.

SMOKED SALMON AND CREAM CHEESE ROLL-UPS

24

Prep Time: 5 minutes | Total Time: 5 minutes | Yield: 2 servings
Nutritional Breakdown (Estimated per serving): Calories: 400 kcal, Protein: 30 g, Fat: 35 g, Carbs: 2 g

Ingredients:
- 4 oz smoked salmon
- 2 tbsp cream cheese
- Salt to taste

Instructions:
1. Prepare Roll-Ups: Spread cream cheese over slices of smoked salmon and roll them up.
2. Serve: Serve cold with a pinch of salt.

GRILLED LAMB CHOPS WITH GARLIC BUTTER

Prep Time: 5 minutes | Cook Time: 15 minutes | Total Time: 20 minutes | Yield: 2 servings
Nutritional Breakdown (Estimated per serving): Calories: 600 kcal, Protein: 45 g, Fat: 50 g, Carbs: 0 g

Ingredients:
- 4 lamb chops
- 2 tbsp butter
- 2 garlic cloves, minced
- Salt to taste

Instructions:
1. Grill Lamb Chops: Heat a skillet over medium-high heat. Grill lamb chops for 4-5 minutes per side until browned.
2. Add Garlic Butter: Lower the heat, add butter and garlic to the skillet, and baste the chops for 1-2 minutes.
3. Serve: Season with salt and serve.

BAKED CHICKEN THIGHS WITH MOZZARELLA

Prep Time: 5 minutes | Cook Time: 20 minutes | Total Time: 25 minutes | Yield: 4 servings
Nutritional Breakdown (Estimated per serving): Calories: 550 kcal, Protein: 40 g, Fat: 45 g, Carbs: 1 g

Ingredients:
- 4 chicken thighs, skin-on
- 1/4 cup shredded mozzarella
- Salt to taste

Instructions:
1. Bake Chicken: Preheat oven to 375°F. Place chicken thighs in a baking dish, season with salt, and bake for 15 minutes.
2. Add Mozzarella: Sprinkle mozzarella on top and bake for another 5 minutes until melted and bubbly.
3. Serve: Serve hot.

BISON STEAKS WITH BONE BROTH REDUCTION

Prep Time: 5 minutes | Cook Time: 15 minutes | Total Time: 20 minutes | Yield: 2 servings
Nutritional Breakdown (Estimated per serving): Calories: 600 kcal, Protein: 50 g, Fat: 40 g, Carbs: 0 g

Ingredients:
- 2 bison steaks
- 1 cup bone broth
- Salt to taste

Instructions:
1. Sear Steaks: Heat a skillet over medium-high heat and sear bison steaks for 4-5 minutes per side.
2. Reduce Broth: Add bone broth to the skillet and reduce for 5 minutes until thickened.
3. Serve: Season with salt and serve with the reduction sauce.

PORK LOIN WITH PARMESAN CRUST

Prep Time: 5 minutes | Cook Time: 20 minutes | Total Time: 25 minutes | Yield: 2 servings
Nutritional Breakdown (Estimated per serving): Calories: 650 kcal, Protein: 45 g, Fat: 55 g, Carbs: 1 g

Ingredients:
- 1 lb pork loin
- 1/4 cup grated parmesan cheese
- Salt to taste

Instructions:
1. Prepare Pork: Preheat oven to 375°F. Rub pork loin with salt and press grated parmesan onto the top.
2. Bake: Bake for 20 minutes, or until the pork is cooked through and the cheese is golden and crispy.
3. Serve: Let rest for a minute before slicing and serving.

PORK CHOPS WITH CRISPY SKIN

Prep Time: 5 minutes | Cook Time: 15 minutes | Total Time: 20 minutes | Yield: 2 servings
Nutritional Breakdown (Estimated per serving): Calories: 600 kcal, Protein: 40 g, Fat: 50 g, Carbs: 0 g

Ingredients:
- 2 bone-in pork chops, skin-on
- Salt to taste
- 2 tbsp tallow or lard

Instructions:
1. Cook Pork Chops: Heat tallow in a skillet over medium-high heat. Add pork chops skin-side down and cook for 6-7 minutes until the skin is crispy. Flip and cook the other side for an additional 5-7 minutes, depending on thickness.
2. Rest and Serve: Let the pork chops rest for a minute before slicing. Season with salt and serve hot.

GRILLED BEEF TONGUE WITH MUSTARD SAUCE   27

Prep Time: 10 minutes | Cook Time: 20 minutes | Total Time: 30 minutes | Yield: 4 servings
Nutritional Breakdown (Estimated per serving): Calories: 600 kcal, Protein: 45 g, Fat: 50 g, Carbs: 0 g

Ingredients:
- 1 lb beef tongue, boiled and sliced
- 2 tbsp mustard
- 2 tbsp beef tallow
- Salt to taste

Instructions:
1. Grill Beef Tongue: Heat a grill or skillet over medium-high heat. Sear the sliced beef tongue for 4-5 minutes per side until browned and crispy.
2. Prepare Mustard Sauce: In a small bowl, mix the mustard with a bit of salt.
Serve: Drizzle the mustard sauce over the grilled beef tongue and serve.

SEARED VENISON STEAKS WITH HERB REDUCTION

Prep Time: 5 minutes | Cook Time: 15 minutes | Total Time: 20 minutes | Yield: 2 servings
Nutritional Breakdown (Estimated per serving): Calories: 500 kcal, Protein: 45 g, Fat: 35 g, Carbs: 0 g

Ingredients:
- 2 venison steaks
- 2 tbsp beef tallow
- 1/2 cup bone broth
- 1 tbsp chopped fresh herbs (e.g., rosemary, thyme)
- Salt to taste

Instructions:
1. Sear Venison: Heat tallow in a skillet over medium-high heat. Sear venison steaks for 4-5 minutes per side for medium-rare doneness.
2. Herb Reduction: Add bone broth and herbs to the pan. Reduce heat and simmer for 5 minutes until the broth thickens slightly.
3. Serve: Season steaks with salt and drizzle the herb reduction over the top before serving.

CHAPTER 4 DINNER
CREAMY CHICKEN THIGHS WITH RICOTTA

Prep Time: 10 minutes | Cook Time: 20 minutes | Total Time: 30 minutes | Yield: 4 servings
Nutritional Breakdown (Estimated per serving): Calories: 600 kcal, Protein: 40 g, Fat: 50 g, Carbs: 2 g

Ingredients:
- 4 chicken thighs, skin-on
- 1/2 cup ricotta cheese
- 2 tbsp butter
- Salt and pepper to taste

Instructions:
1. Cook Chicken: Heat butter in a skillet over medium-high heat. Cook chicken thighs skin-side down for 10 minutes until crispy, then flip and cook for another 8 minutes.
2. Add Ricotta: Lower heat, spread ricotta cheese on top of the thighs, and cook for an additional 2 minutes.
3. Serve: Season with salt and pepper.

PAN-SEARED BARRAMUNDI WITH HERB BUTTER

Prep Time: 5 minutes | Cook Time: 10 minutes | Total Time: 15 minutes | Yield: 2 servings
Nutritional Breakdown (Estimated per serving): Calories: 500 kcal, Protein: 40 g, Fat: 35 g, Carbs: 0 g

Ingredients:
- 2 barramundi fillets
- 2 tbsp butter
- 1 tbsp fresh parsley, chopped
- 1 clove garlic, minced
- Salt to taste

Instructions:
1. Sear Barramundi: Heat butter in a skillet over medium-high heat. Sear the barramundi fillets for 3-4 minutes per side, until the skin is crispy and the fish is cooked through.
2. Add Herbs and Garlic: Lower the heat, add garlic and parsley, and cook for an additional 1-2 minutes, letting the flavors combine.
3. Serve: Season with salt and serve hot.

SEARED BEEF HEART WITH GARLIC BUTTER

Prep Time: 5 minutes | **Cook Time:** 15 minutes | **Total Time:** 20 minutes | **Yield:** 4 servings
Nutritional Breakdown (Estimated per serving): Calories: 500 kcal, Protein: 40 g, Fat: 35 g, Carbs: 0 g

Ingredients:
- 1 lb beef heart, sliced
- 2 tbsp tallow
- 2 cloves garlic, minced
- Salt to taste

Instructions:
1. Sear Beef Heart: Heat tallow in a skillet over medium-high heat. Add sliced beef heart and cook for 10 minutes until browned.
2. Add Garlic: Lower the heat, add garlic, and cook for an additional 2-3 minutes.
3. Serve: Season with salt.

GRILLED PORK RIBS WITH BONE BROTH GLAZE

Prep Time: 10 minutes | **Cook Time:** 20 minutes | **Total Time:** 30 minutes | **Yield:** 4 servings
Nutritional Breakdown (Estimated per serving): Calories: 700 kcal, Protein: 45 g, Fat: 60 g, Carbs: 0 g

Ingredients:
- 2 lbs pork ribs
- 1 cup bone broth
- Salt and pepper to taste

Instructions:
1. Grill Ribs: Preheat a grill to medium heat. Grill pork ribs for 15-20 minutes, turning occasionally, until fully cooked.
2. Bone Broth Glaze: In the last 5 minutes of grilling, brush the ribs with bone broth and continue grilling until the glaze thickens.
3. Serve: Season with salt and pepper.

VENISON STEAK WITH MUSHROOM SAUCE

Prep Time: 10 minutes | **Cook Time:** 15 minutes | **Total Time:** 25 minutes | **Yield:** 2 servings
Nutritional Breakdown (Estimated per serving): Calories: 500 kcal, Protein: 45 g, Fat: 35 g, Carbs: 1 g

Ingredients:
- 2 venison steaks
- 1 cup mushrooms, sliced
- 1 tbsp tallow (or butter)
- Salt to taste

Instructions:
1. Sear Steaks: Heat tallow in a skillet over medium-high heat. Season venison steaks with salt and sear for 4-5 minutes per side until desired doneness. Remove and let rest.
2. Cook Mushrooms: In the same skillet, cook mushrooms for 5-7 minutes until browned.
3. Serve: Top the venison steaks with the sautéed mushrooms and serve hot.

BAKED BEEF SHORT RIBS WITH TALLOW

Prep Time: 5 minutes | **Cook Time:** 25 minutes | **Total Time:** 30 minutes | **Yield:** 4 servings
Nutritional Breakdown (Estimated per serving): Calories: 700 kcal, Protein: 50 g, Fat: 60 g, Carbs: 0 g

Ingredients:
- 2 lbs beef short ribs
- 2 tbsp tallow
- Salt to taste

Instructions:
1. Sear Short Ribs: Preheat oven to 375°F. Heat tallow in a skillet over medium-high heat and sear short ribs for 5 minutes per side.
2. Bake: Transfer the short ribs to the oven and bake for 20 minutes until fully tender.
3. Serve: Season with salt and serve.

LAMB SHANK WITH FENNEL AND GARLIC

Prep Time: 10 minutes | Cook Time: 30 minutes | Total Time: 40 minutes | Yield: 4 servings
Nutritional Breakdown (Estimated per serving): Calories: 650 kcal, Protein: 45 g, Fat: 55 g, Carbs: 2 g

Ingredients:
- 2 lamb shanks
- 1 bulb fennel, sliced
- 2 cloves garlic, minced
- 2 tbsp tallow
- Salt to taste

Instructions:
1. Sear Lamb Shanks: Heat tallow in a skillet over medium-high heat. Sear lamb shanks for 5 minutes on each side.
2. Cook with Fennel: Lower heat, add sliced fennel and garlic, and cook for 20-25 minutes, stirring occasionally.
Serve: Season with salt and serve.

BISON MEATBALLS WITH BONE BROTH GRAVY

Prep Time: 10 minutes | Cook Time: 20 minutes | Total Time: 30 minutes | Yield: 4 servings
Nutritional Breakdown (Estimated per serving): Calories: 600 kcal, Protein: 40 g, Fat: 50 g, Carbs: 0 g

Ingredients:
- 1 lb ground bison
- 1/2 cup crushed pork rinds
- 1 cup bone broth
- 1 tbsp tallow
- Salt to taste

Instructions:
1. Form Meatballs: In a bowl, mix ground bison with crushed pork rinds and form into meatballs.
2. Cook Meatballs: Heat tallow in a skillet over medium heat and cook the meatballs for 10-12 minutes until browned and cooked through.
3. Make Gravy: Pour bone broth into the skillet and simmer for 5-7 minutes until thickened into a gravy.
4. Serve: Season with salt and serve meatballs with bone broth gravy.

PAN-SEARED RABBIT WITH THYME AND GARLIC

Prep Time: 5 minutes | Cook Time: 15 minutes | Total Time: 20 minutes | Yield: 4 servings
Nutritional Breakdown (Estimated per serving): Calories: 500 kcal, Protein: 45 g, Fat: 35 g, Carbs: 0 g

Ingredients:
- 1 whole rabbit, cut into pieces
- 2 tbsp tallow or lard
- 1 tbsp fresh thyme
- 2 cloves garlic, minced
- Salt to taste

Instructions:
1. Sear Rabbit: Heat tallow in a skillet over medium-high heat. Sear the rabbit pieces for 5-6 minutes per side until browned and cooked through.
2. Add Garlic and Thyme: Lower heat, add garlic and thyme, and cook for another 2-3 minutes to infuse the flavors.
3. Serve: Season with salt and serve hot.

PORK BELLY SKEWERS

Prep Time: 5 minutes | Cook Time: 20 minutes | Total Time: 25 minutes | Yield: 4 servings
Nutritional Breakdown (Estimated per serving): Calories: 700 kcal, Protein: 40 g, Fat: 60 g, Carbs: 0 g

Ingredients:
- 1 lb pork belly, cubed
- Salt to taste

Instructions:
1. Prepare Skewers: Thread the cubed pork belly onto metal or wooden skewers. Season generously with salt.
2. Cook Pork Belly: Heat a grill or large skillet over medium-high heat. Grill or pan-fry the skewers for 20 minutes, turning occasionally, until crispy and golden brown on all sides.
3. Serve: Serve hot with additional salt if desired.

PORK TENDERLOIN WITH GHEE

33

Prep Time: 5 minutes | **Cook Time:** 15 minutes | **Total Time:** 20 minutes | **Yield:** 4 servings
Nutritional Breakdown (Estimated per serving): Calories: 550 kcal, Protein: 45 g, Fat: 40 g, Carbs: 0 g

Ingredients:
- 1 lb pork tenderloin
- 2 tbsp ghee
- Salt to taste

Instructions:
1. Cook Tenderloin: Heat ghee in a skillet over medium-high heat. Sear the pork tenderloin for 7-8 minutes on each side until fully cooked and browned.
2. Serve: Season with salt and serve hot.

VEAL CUTLETS WITH GHEE

Prep Time: 5 minutes | **Cook Time:** 10 minutes | **Total Time:** 15 minutes | **Yield:** 4 servings
Nutritional Breakdown (Estimated per serving): Calories: 500 kcal, Protein: 40 g, Fat: 35 g, Carbs: 0 g

Ingredients:
- 1 lb veal cutlets
- 2 tbsp ghee
- Salt and pepper to taste

Instructions:
1. Cook Cutlets: Heat ghee in a skillet over medium-high heat. Sear the veal cutlets for 3-4 minutes per side until browned and cooked through.
2. Serve: Season with salt and pepper, and serve hot.

BISON STEAK WITH HERB BUTTER

Prep Time: 5 minutes | Cook Time: 10 minutes | Total Time: 15 minutes | Yield: 4 servings
Nutritional Breakdown (Estimated per serving): Calories: 550 kcal, Protein: 45 g, Fat: 40 g, Carbs: 0 g

Ingredients:
- 1 lb bison steak
- 2 tbsp butter
- 1 tsp thyme, chopped
- Salt to taste

Instructions:
1. Cook Steak: Heat butter in a skillet over high heat. Sear the bison steaks for 4-5 minutes on each side until cooked to your liking.
2. Serve: Season with thyme and salt, and serve.

CARNIVORE SUSHI ROLLS

Prep Time: 10 minutes | Total Time: 10 minutes | Yield: 4 servings
Nutritional Breakdown (Estimated per serving): Calories: 400 kcal, Protein: 35 g, Fat: 30 g, Carbs: 1 g

Ingredients:
- 8 slices thinly sliced roast beef or smoked salmon (as the "nori" wrap)
- 1/2 lb cooked shrimp, crab, or tuna (for filling)
- 4 oz cream cheese, softened
- 1 tbsp beef tallow or butter (optional for brushing)
- Salt to taste

Instructions:
1. Prepare Wrap: Lay the roast beef or smoked salmon slices flat on a clean surface.
2. Add Filling: Spread a thin layer of cream cheese on each slice. Place a few pieces of shrimp, crab, or tuna in the center.
3. Roll: Carefully roll up each slice, tucking in the filling as you go to create a tight roll.
4. Optional Sear: If desired, lightly sear the rolls in a hot skillet with a bit of beef tallow or butter for 1-2 minutes for extra flavor and texture.
5. Serve: Slice into bite-sized sushi rolls and serve immediately.

STUFFED CHICKEN THIGHS WITH BACON

Prep Time: 10 minutes | Cook Time: 20 minutes | Total Time: 30 minutes | Yield: 2 servings
Nutritional Breakdown (Estimated per serving): Calories: 550 kcal, Protein: 40 g, Fat: 45 g, Carbs: 1 g

Ingredients:
- 4 boneless chicken thighs
- 4 slices bacon
- 4 oz cream cheese, softened
- Salt and pepper to taste

Instructions:
1. Preheat Oven: Preheat your oven to 375°F (190°C).
2. Prepare Chicken: Season the chicken thighs with salt and pepper. Spread a layer of cream cheese on the inside of each thigh.
3. Wrap with Bacon: Roll up each chicken thigh and wrap it tightly with a slice of bacon.
4. Sear and Bake: In a hot skillet, sear the bacon-wrapped chicken thighs for 2-3 minutes on each side until browned. Transfer to a baking dish and bake for 15-20 minutes until fully cooked.
5. Serve: Let rest for a few minutes before serving.

GRILLED BEEF KEBABS WITH BACON

Prep Time: 10 minutes | Cook Time: 10 minutes | Total Time: 20 minutes | Yield: 4 servings
Nutritional Breakdown (Estimated per serving): Calories: 700 kcal, Protein: 45 g, Fat: 55 g, Carbs: 0 g

Ingredients:
- 1 lb beef sirloin, cubed
- 8 slices bacon, cut into halves
- Salt to taste

Instructions:
1. Assemble Kebabs: Wrap each beef cube with a piece of bacon and thread them onto metal or wooden skewers.
2. Cook Kebabs: Heat a grill or skillet over medium-high heat. Cook the kebabs for 8-10 minutes, turning occasionally, until the bacon is crispy and the beef is fully cooked.
3. Serve: Season with salt and serve.

CHAPTER 5 SOUPS AND STEWS

CHICKEN & DUCK FAT SOUP

Prep Time: 5 minutes | Cook Time: 20 minutes | Total Time: 25 minutes | Yield: 4 servings
Nutritional Breakdown (Estimated per serving): Calories: 600 kcal, Protein: 50 g, Fat: 50 g, Carbs: 0 g

Ingredients:
- 1 lb chicken thighs, boneless
- 4 cups chicken bone broth
- 2 tbsp duck fat
- Salt to taste

Instructions:
1. Sear Chicken: Heat duck fat in a pot over medium heat. Once the fat is hot, add the chicken thighs and sear for 5-6 minutes per side until golden brown.
2. Simmer in Broth: Pour in the chicken bone broth. Bring to a gentle boil, then lower heat to simmer for 15 minutes, ensuring the chicken is cooked through and tender.
3. Serve: Season with salt to taste, and serve hot.

PORK BELLY AND BEEF HEART STEW

Prep Time: 5 minutes | Cook Time: 25 minutes | Total Time: 30 minutes | Yield: 4 servings
Nutritional Breakdown (Estimated per serving): Calories: 800 kcal, Protein: 65 g, Fat: 70 g, Carbs: 0 g

Ingredients:
- 1/2 lb pork belly, cubed
- 1/2 lb beef heart, thinly sliced
- 4 cups beef broth
- 2 tbsp tallow
- Salt to taste

Instructions:
1. Brown Pork Belly: Heat tallow in a large pot over medium-high heat. Add cubed pork belly and cook for 8-10 minutes, stirring occasionally, until it becomes crispy and golden.
2. Add Beef Heart: Add the beef heart slices to the pot and cook for an additional 5 minutes, stirring often, until the heart is browned.
3. Simmer in Broth: Pour in the beef broth, bring to a simmer, and cook for 10-12 minutes until the meats are tender and flavorful.
4. Serve: Season with salt to taste, and serve immediately.

CARNIVORE SEAFOOD SOUP

Prep Time: 5 minutes | **Cook Time:** 20 minutes | **Total Time:** 25 minutes | **Yield:** 4 servings
Nutritional Breakdown (Estimated per serving): Calories: 600 kcal, Protein: 50 g, Fat: 40 g, Carbs: 0 g

Ingredients:
- 1 lb shrimp, peeled and deveined
- 4 oz cod, cubed
- 4 cups fish broth
- 2 tbsp butter
- Salt to taste

Instructions:
1. Cook Seafood: Melt butter in a large pot over medium heat. Add the shrimp and cod, and cook for 5-7 minutes until the seafood is fully opaque and cooked through.
2. Add Broth: Pour in the fish broth and bring to a gentle boil. Lower the heat and simmer for 10-12 minutes to allow the seafood flavors to infuse into the broth.
3. Serve: Season with salt to taste and serve hot.

DUCK BREAST AND BEEF BROTH SOUP

Prep Time: 5 minutes | **Cook Time:** 20 minutes | **Total Time:** 25 minutes | **Yield:** 4 servings
Nutritional Breakdown (Estimated per serving): Calories: 700 kcal, Protein: 55 g, Fat: 60 g, Carbs: 0 g

Ingredients:
- 2 duck breasts, skin-on
- 4 cups beef broth
- 2 tbsp duck fat
Salt to taste

Instructions:
1. Sear Duck Breasts: Heat duck fat in a pot over medium heat. Place the duck breasts skin-side down and sear for 6-8 minutes until the skin is crispy. Flip and cook for another 4-5 minutes until cooked through.
2. Simmer in Broth: Remove the duck breasts and slice them thinly. Return the slices to the pot, add beef broth, and simmer for 10 minutes to meld the flavors.
3. Serve: Season with salt and serve hot.

LOBSTER AND SHRIMP STEW

Prep Time: 5 minutes | **Cook Time:** 20 minutes | **Total Time:** 25 minutes | **Yield:** 4 servings
Nutritional Breakdown (Estimated per serving): Calories: 700 kcal, Protein: 60 g, Fat: 50 g, Carbs: 0 g

Ingredients:
- 1 lobster tail, diced
- 1/2 lb shrimp, peeled and deveined
- 4 cups fish bone broth
- 2 tbsp butter
- Salt to taste

Instructions:
1. Sear Lobster and Shrimp: Heat butter in a large pot over medium heat. Add diced lobster tail and shrimp, cooking for 5-6 minutes until the seafood is cooked through.
2. Add Broth: Pour in the fish bone broth and bring to a gentle simmer. Cook for an additional 10 minutes, allowing the flavors to meld.
3. Serve: Season with salt and serve hot.

CHAPTER 6 SEAFOOD AND FISH
LOBSTER TAIL WITH GARLIC BUTTER

Prep Time: 5 minutes | **Cook Time:** 15 minutes | **Total Time:** 20 minutes | **Yield:** 2 servings
Nutritional Breakdown (Estimated per serving): Calories: 500 kcal, Protein: 40 g, Fat: 40 g, Carbs: 0 g

Ingredients:
- 2 lobster tails, split
- 2 tbsp butter
- 2 garlic cloves, minced
- Salt to taste

Instructions:
1. Sear Lobster: Heat butter in a skillet over medium heat. Add the lobster tails and sear, shell-side down, for 5-6 minutes.
2. Add Garlic: Add minced garlic and cook for another 4-5 minutes, basting the lobster meat with the garlic butter.
3. Serve: Season with salt and serve hot.

GRILLED SHRIMP WITH LEMON BUTTER

Prep Time: 5 minutes | **Cook Time:** 10 minutes | **Total Time:** 15 minutes | **Yield:** 2 servings
Nutritional Breakdown (Estimated per serving): Calories: 400 kcal, Protein: 35 g, Fat: 30 g, Carbs: 0 g

Ingredients:
- 1 lb shrimp, peeled and deveined
- 2 tbsp butter
- 1 tsp lemon juice
- Salt to taste

Instructions:
1. Cook Shrimp: Heat butter in a skillet over medium-high heat. Add shrimp and cook for 3-4 minutes per side until opaque.
2. Add Lemon: Drizzle lemon juice over the shrimp and stir for another minute.
3. Serve: Season with salt and serve hot.

SEARED TUNA WITH AVOCADO

Prep Time: 5 minutes | Cook Time: 10 minutes | Total Time: 15 minutes | Yield: 2 servings
Nutritional Breakdown (Estimated per serving): Calories: 600 kcal, Protein: 40 g, Fat: 50 g, Carbs: 0 g

Ingredients:
- 2 tuna steaks
- 1/2 avocado, sliced
- 2 tbsp ghee
- Salt to taste

Instructions:
1. Sear Tuna: Heat ghee in a skillet over medium-high heat. Sear the tuna steaks for 2-3 minutes per side for medium-rare, or longer for well-done.
2. Add Avocado: Plate the tuna steaks and top with avocado slices.
3. Serve: Season with salt and serve hot.

GRILLED SWORDFISH WITH HERB BUTTER

Prep Time: 5 minutes | Cook Time: 15 minutes | Total Time: 20 minutes | Yield: 2 servings
Nutritional Breakdown (Estimated per serving): Calories: 600 kcal, Protein: 50 g, Fat: 45 g, Carbs: 0 g

Ingredients:
- 2 swordfish steaks
- 2 tbsp butter
- 1 tsp fresh herbs (thyme or rosemary)
- Salt to taste

Instructions:
1. Grill Swordfish: Heat a grill or skillet over medium-high heat. Grill the swordfish steaks for 5-6 minutes on each side.
2. Add Herb Butter: Melt butter in a small pan and stir in fresh herbs. Drizzle over the swordfish.
3. Serve: Season with salt and serve hot.

PAN-FRIED SALMON WITH DILL

Prep Time: 5 minutes | Cook Time: 10 minutes | Total Time: 15 minutes | Yield: 2 servings
Nutritional Breakdown (Estimated per serving): Calories: 500 kcal, Protein: 40 g, Fat: 40 g, Carbs: 0 g

Ingredients:
- 2 salmon fillets
- 2 tbsp butter
- 1 tsp fresh dill
- Salt to taste

Instructions:
1. Sear Salmon: Heat butter in a skillet over medium heat. Add the salmon fillets skin-side down and cook for 4-5 minutes until crispy.
2. Flip and Add Dill: Flip the fillets, add fresh dill, and cook for another 2-3 minutes.
3. Serve: Season with salt and serve hot.

BAKED COD WITH OLIVE OIL AND HERBS

Prep Time: 5 minutes | Cook Time: 15 minutes | Total Time: 20 minutes | Yield: 2 servings
Nutritional Breakdown (Estimated per serving): Calories: 450 kcal, Protein: 40 g, Fat: 35 g, Carbs: 0 g

Ingredients:
- 2 cod fillets
- 2 tbsp olive oil
- 1 tsp thyme or rosemary
- Salt to taste

Instructions:
1. Prepare Cod: Preheat your oven to 400°F. Place cod fillets in a greased baking dish and drizzle with olive oil.
2. Add Herbs: Sprinkle fresh herbs and salt over the fish.
3. Bake: Bake for 12-15 minutes until the fish is flaky.
4. Serve: Serve hot.

GRILLED OCTOPUS WITH OLIVE OIL

Prep Time: 5 minutes | Cook Time: 20 minutes | Total Time: 25 minutes | Yield: 2 servings
Nutritional Breakdown (Estimated per serving): Calories: 500 kcal, Protein: 40 g, Fat: 40 g, Carbs: 0 g

Ingredients:
- 1/2 lb octopus tentacles
- 2 tbsp olive oil
- Salt to taste

Instructions:
1. Boil Octopus: Bring a pot of water to boil and cook the octopus tentacles for 10 minutes until tender.
2. Grill Octopus: Heat olive oil in a skillet or grill over medium-high heat. Grill the tentacles for 4-5 minutes on each side until slightly charred.
3. Serve: Season with salt and serve hot.

SCALLOP AND SHRIMP STEW

Prep Time: 5 minutes | Cook Time: 20 minutes | Total Time: 25 minutes | Yield: 4 servings
Nutritional Breakdown (Estimated per serving): Calories: 600 kcal, Protein: 50 g, Fat: 50 g, Carbs: 0 g

Ingredients:
- 1/2 lb scallops
- 1/2 lb shrimp, peeled and deveined
- 4 cups fish broth
- 2 tbsp butter
- Salt to taste

Instructions:
1. Sear Scallops and Shrimp: Heat butter in a pot over medium heat. Add scallops and shrimp and cook for 5-6 minutes until lightly browned.
2. Add Broth: Pour in the fish broth and simmer for 10-15 minutes.
3. Serve: Season with salt and serve hot.

GRILLED MACKEREL WITH GARLIC

Prep Time: 5 minutes | **Cook Time:** 10 minutes | **Total Time:** 15 minutes | **Yield:** 2 servings
Nutritional Breakdown (Estimated per serving): Calories: 500 kcal, Protein: 40 g, Fat: 40 g, Carbs: 0 g

Ingredients:
- 2 mackerel fillets
- 2 garlic cloves, minced
- 2 tbsp olive oil
- Salt to taste

Instructions:
1. Grill Mackerel: Heat olive oil in a skillet over medium heat. Add the mackerel fillets, skin-side down, and cook for 5-6 minutes until the skin is crispy.
2. Add Garlic: Flip the fillets, add minced garlic, and cook for another 2-3 minutes until the fish is fully cooked and garlic is fragrant.
3. Serve: Season with salt and serve hot.

SEARED SCALLOPS WITH OLIVE OIL

Prep Time: 5 minutes | **Cook Time:** 10 minutes | **Total Time:** 15 minutes | **Yield:** 2 servings
Nutritional Breakdown (Estimated per serving): Calories: 450 kcal, Protein: 35 g, Fat: 35 g, Carbs: 0 g

Ingredients:
- 8 large scallops
- 2 tbsp olive oil
- Salt to taste

Instructions:
1. Sear Scallops: Heat olive oil in a skillet over high heat. Add scallops and sear for 2-3 minutes on each side until golden brown.
2. Serve: Season with salt and serve hot.

GRILLED CALAMARI WITH OLIVE OIL

Prep Time: 5 minutes | **Cook Time:** 10 minutes | **Total Time:** 15 minutes | **Yield:** 2 servings
Nutritional Breakdown (Estimated per serving): Calories: 400 kcal, Protein: 35 g, Fat: 30 g, Carbs: 0 g

Ingredients:
- 1/2 lb calamari, cleaned and sliced
- 2 tbsp olive oil
- Salt to taste

Instructions:
1. Grill Calamari: Heat olive oil in a skillet over medium-high heat. Add calamari slices and grill for 4-5 minutes until they become slightly crispy.
2. Serve: Season with salt and serve hot.

GRILLED SARDINES WITH GARLIC AND HERB BUTTER

Prep Time: 5 minutes | **Cook Time:** 10 minutes | **Total Time:** 15 minutes | **Yield:** 2 servings
Nutritional Breakdown (Estimated per serving): Calories: 450 kcal, Protein: 35 g, Fat: 35 g, Carbs: 0 g

Ingredients:
- 6 whole sardines, cleaned
- 2 tbsp butter
- 1 garlic clove, minced
- 1 tsp fresh parsley, chopped
- Salt to taste

Instructions:
1. Grill Sardines: Heat a grill pan or skillet over medium-high heat. Grill the sardines for 4-5 minutes on each side until crispy and cooked through.
2. Make Herb Butter: Melt butter in a small pan, add minced garlic and parsley, and cook for 1-2 minutes until fragrant.
3. Serve: Drizzle the garlic herb butter over the sardines, season with salt, and serve hot.

SEARED HALIBUT WITH CAPER BUTTER SAUCE

Prep Time: 5 minutes | Cook Time: 10 minutes | Total Time: 15 minutes | Yield: 2 servings
Nutritional Breakdown (Estimated per serving): Calories: 450 kcal, Protein: 40 g, Fat: 35 g, Carbs: 0 g

Ingredients:
- 2 halibut fillets
- 2 tbsp butter
- 1 tbsp capers
- 1 tsp lemon juice
- Salt to taste

Instructions:
1. Sear Halibut: Heat butter in a skillet over medium-high heat. Add halibut fillets and cook for 4-5 minutes on each side until golden and cooked through.
2. Make Caper Sauce: In the same skillet, add capers and lemon juice to the remaining butter and cook for 1-2 minutes.
3. Serve: Drizzle the caper butter sauce over the halibut, season with salt, and serve.

GRILLED PRAWNS WITH GARLIC AND LEMON

Prep Time: 5 minutes | Cook Time: 10 minutes | Total Time: 15 minutes | Yield: 2 servings
Nutritional Breakdown (Estimated per serving): Calories: 500 kcal, Protein: 40 g, Fat: 35 g, Carbs: 0 g

Ingredients:
- 1 lb large prawns, peeled and deveined
- 2 tbsp olive oil
- 1 garlic clove, minced
- 1 tsp lemon juice
- Salt to taste

Instructions:
1. Grill Prawns: Heat olive oil in a skillet over medium-high heat. Add prawns and cook for 3-4 minutes on each side until fully cooked.
2. Add Garlic and Lemon: During the last minute of cooking, add minced garlic and lemon juice, stirring for 1-2 minutes.
3. Serve: Season with salt and serve hot.

CHAPTER 7 SNACKS
PORK RIND NACHOS

Prep Time: 5 minutes | Total Time: 5 minutes | Yield: 2 servings
Nutritional Breakdown (Estimated per serving): Calories: 400 kcal, Protein: 25 g, Fat: 30 g, Carbs: 0 g

Ingredients:
- 2 cups pork rinds
- 1/2 cup shredded cheddar cheese
- 1/4 cup sour cream (optional)

Instructions:
1. Prepare Nachos: Lay the pork rinds evenly on a microwave-safe plate, making sure they don't overlap too much to allow for even melting.
2. Add Cheese: Sprinkle the shredded cheddar cheese evenly over the pork rinds.
3. Melt Cheese: Microwave for 30-45 seconds or until the cheese is fully melted and bubbly. Watch closely to prevent overcooking.
4. Serve: Serve immediately with a dollop of sour cream on the side if desired.

CARNIVORE MEAT CHIPS

Prep Time: 5 minutes | Cook Time: 15 minutes | Total Time: 20 minutes
Nutritional Breakdown (Estimated per serving): Calories: 180 kcal, Fat: 10 g, Protein: 20 g, Carbs: 0 g Yield: 4 servings

Ingredients:
- 1/2 lb thinly sliced roast beef or turkey deli meat
- Salt to taste
- Optional: garlic powder or smoked paprika for seasoning

Instructions:
1. Preheat Oven: Preheat your oven to 375°F (190°C) and line a baking sheet with parchment paper.
2. Prepare Meat: Lay the thin slices of roast beef or turkey flat on the baking sheet. Sprinkle with salt and any optional seasonings.
3. Bake: Bake in the preheated oven for 10-15 minutes, or until the slices are crispy and golden brown.
4. Cool and Serve: Let the meat chips cool for a few minutes to become even crispier, then serve.

BACON-WRAPPED AVOCADO BITES

Prep Time: 5 minutes | **Cook Time:** 10 minutes | **Total Time:** 15 minutes | **Yield:** 4 servings
Nutritional Breakdown (Estimated per serving): Calories: 350 kcal, Protein: 20 g, Fat: 30 g, Carbs: 1 g

Ingredients:
- 2 avocados, sliced into wedges
- 8 slices bacon

Instructions:
1. Prepare Avocado: Slice each avocado into 6-8 wedges, ensuring they are thick enough to hold the bacon wrap.
2. Wrap Avocados: Take a bacon slice and wrap it tightly around each avocado wedge.
3. Fry Bacon-Wrapped Avocados: Heat a skillet over medium heat. Place the bacon-wrapped avocado wedges in the skillet and cook for 8-10 minutes, turning them occasionally to ensure the bacon is evenly crispy on all sides.
4. Drain and Serve: Remove from the skillet and place on paper towels to drain any excess grease. Serve warm.

CHEDDAR CHEESE CHIPS

Prep Time: 5 minutes | **Cook Time:** 10 minutes | **Total Time:** 15 minutes | **Yield:** 4 servings
Nutritional Breakdown (Estimated per serving): Calories: 350 kcal, Protein: 20 g, Fat: 30 g, Carbs: 1 g

Ingredients:
- 1 cup shredded cheddar cheese

Instructions:
1. Preheat Oven: Preheat your oven to 375°F.
2. Prepare Cheese Mounds: On a parchment-lined baking sheet, place small piles (about 1 tablespoon each) of shredded cheddar cheese. Make sure to space them at least 1 inch apart as they will spread.
3. Bake the Cheese: Bake for 8-10 minutes or until the cheese is melted and the edges are turning crispy and golden.
4. Cool: Remove from the oven and allow the cheese chips to cool on the tray for about 5 minutes to firm up.
5. Serve: Carefully lift the cooled cheese chips from the parchment and serve.

DEVILED EGGS

Prep Time: 10 minutes | Cook Time: 10 minutes | Total Time: 20 minutes | Yield: 4 servings
Nutritional Breakdown (Estimated per serving): Calories: 200 kcal, Protein: 12 g, Fat: 18 g, Carbs: 0 g

Ingredients:
- 6 hard-boiled eggs
- 2 tbsp mayonnaise
- Salt to taste

Instructions:
1. Boil and Peel Eggs: Boil the eggs in a pot of water for 10 minutes. Cool the eggs under cold water, peel, and cut them in half lengthwise.
2. Prepare Yolk Mixture: Remove the yolks from the eggs and place them in a small bowl. Mash the yolks with a fork and mix in mayonnaise until smooth. Add salt to taste.
3. Fill the Egg Whites: Spoon or pipe the yolk mixture back into the hollowed egg whites.
4. Serve: Serve as a quick snack or appetizer.

PEPPERONI CHIPS

Prep Time: 5 minutes | Cook Time: 10 minutes | Total Time: 15 minutes | Yield: 4 servings
Nutritional Breakdown (Estimated per serving): Calories: 250 kcal, Protein: 20 g, Fat: 20 g, Carbs: 0 g

Ingredients:
- 1 cup pepperoni slices

Instructions:
1. Preheat Oven: Preheat your oven to 375°F.
2. Prepare Pepperoni: Lay the pepperoni slices in a single layer on a parchment-lined baking sheet.
3. Bake: Bake for 8-10 minutes until the pepperoni slices are crispy.
4. Cool: Let the pepperoni chips cool on the baking sheet for 5 minutes.
5. Serve: Serve immediately or store in an airtight container.

PORK CRACKLINGS

Prep Time: 5 minutes | **Cook Time:** 15 minutes | **Total Time:** 20 minutes | **Yield:** 4 servings
Nutritional Breakdown (Estimated per serving): Calories: 400 kcal, Protein: 30 g, Fat: 35 g, Carbs: 0 g

Ingredients:
- 1 lb pork skin, cut into strips
- Salt to taste

Instructions:
1. Prepare the Pork Skin: Make sure the pork skin is dry before cooking. Pat it with paper towels to remove excess moisture.
2. Fry Pork Skins: Heat a skillet over medium-high heat. Add the pork skin strips and fry for 10-15 minutes, stirring occasionally until crispy and golden brown.
3. Drain and Season: Remove from heat and place the pork cracklings on a paper towel to drain any excess fat. Sprinkle generously with salt while still hot.
4. Serve: Serve immediately for the best crunch.

BACON-WRAPPED SCALLOPS

Prep Time: 5 minutes | **Cook Time:** 10 minutes | **Total Time:** 15 minutes | **Yield:** 4 servings
Nutritional Breakdown (Estimated per serving): Calories: 450 kcal, Protein: 35 g, Fat: 30 g, Carbs: 0 g

Ingredients:
- 12 large scallops
- 12 slices bacon

Instructions:
1. Wrap Scallops: Wrap each scallop with a slice of bacon and secure with a toothpick. Make sure the bacon is snug but not too tight.
2. Fry the Scallops: Heat a skillet over medium heat. Place the bacon-wrapped scallops in the pan and cook for 4-5 minutes on each side, or until the bacon is crispy and the scallops are fully cooked.
Drain and Serve: Drain on paper towels and serve immediately.

DUCK FAT CRISPS

Prep Time: 5 minutes | **Cook Time:** 15 minutes | **Total Time:** 20 minutes
Nutritional Breakdown (Estimated per serving): Calories: 300 kcal, Fat: 28 g, Protein: 12 g, Carbs: 0 g Yield: 4 servings

Ingredients:
- 1 cup duck skin, cut into thin strips
- Salt to taste
- Optional: 1 tsp smoked paprika or garlic powder for seasoning

Instructions:
1. Preheat Oven: Preheat your oven to 400°F (200°C) and line a baking sheet with parchment paper.
2. Prepare Duck Skin: Lay the duck skin strips flat on the baking sheet in a single layer.
3. Bake: Bake for 12-15 minutes, or until the duck skin crisps up and turns golden brown.
4. Season: Remove from the oven and sprinkle with salt. Add optional smoked paprika or garlic powder for extra flavor.
5. Serve: Let cool slightly before serving for the crispiest texture.

TURKEY BACON BITES

Prep Time: 5 minutes | **Cook Time:** 10 minutes | **Total Time:** 15 minutes | **Yield:** 4 servings
Nutritional Breakdown (Estimated per serving): Calories: 300 kcal, Protein: 25 g, Fat: 20 g, Carbs: 0 g

Ingredients:
- 8 slices turkey bacon
- 1/2 lb ground turkey

Instructions:
1. Form Turkey Balls: Form the ground turkey into small balls.
2. Wrap in Bacon: Wrap each turkey ball with a slice of turkey bacon, securing with a toothpick if needed.
3. Cook: Fry in a skillet over medium heat for 8-10 minutes until the turkey bacon is crispy and the ground turkey is cooked through.
4. Serve: Drain on paper towels and serve hot.

CHAPTER 8 SAUCES
SAVORY BEEF DRIPPINGS GRAVY

Prep Time: 5 minutes | Cook Time: 10 minutes | Total Time: 15 minutes
Nutritional Breakdown (Estimated per serving): Calories: 180 kcal, Fat: 16 g, Protein: 2 g, Carbs: 1 g Yield: 4 servings

Ingredients:
- 1/4 cup beef drippings (from cooked steak or roast)
- 1/2 cup beef broth
- 1 tbsp butter
- Pinch of salt
- 1 tsp paprika (optional for color and flavor)

Instructions:
1. Heat Drippings: In a small saucepan over medium heat, add the beef drippings and butter. Allow the mixture to heat until the butter is melted.
2. Add Broth: Stir in the beef broth and paprika (optional for a deeper color and flavor). Simmer the mixture for 5-7 minutes, letting it reduce and thicken slightly.
3. Season and Serve: Add a pinch of salt and serve the rich gravy over steaks, roasts, or even burgers.

BONE BROTH BÉARNAISE SAUCE

Prep Time: 10 minutes | Cook Time: 10 minutes | Total Time: 20 minutes
Nutritional Breakdown (Estimated per serving): Calories: 200 kcal, Fat: 22 g, Protein: 1 g, Carbs: 0 g

Ingredients:
- 1/2 cup butter, melted
- 2 egg yolks
- 1 tbsp bone broth (instead of vinegar)
- 1 tbsp fresh tarragon, chopped
- Salt to taste

Instructions:
1. Prepare Egg Yolks: In a small saucepan over very low heat, whisk together egg yolks and bone broth until smooth.
2. Add Butter: Slowly whisk in melted butter until the sauce is thick and creamy.
3. Add Tarragon: Stir in fresh tarragon and season with salt. Serve over steaks or roasted meats.

ROASTED GARLIC AND TALLOW SAUCE

Prep Time: 10 minutes | **Cook Time:** 15 minutes | **Total Time:** 25 minutes
Nutritional Breakdown (Estimated per serving): Calories: 180 kcal, Fat: 20 g, Protein: 1 g, Carbs: 0 g

Ingredients:
- 1/4 cup beef tallow
- 4 cloves garlic, roasted
- Salt to taste

Instructions:
1. Roast Garlic: Roast garlic cloves in the oven at 400°F for 15 minutes until soft.
2. Melt Tallow: In a saucepan, melt beef tallow over low heat.
3. Combine: Mash roasted garlic into the tallow and whisk until smooth.
4. Serve: Season with salt and serve with grilled meats or as a dip.

CREAMY CARNIVORE GARLIC BUTTER SAUCE

Prep Time: 5 minutes | **Cook Time:** 10 minutes | **Total Time:** 15 minutes
Nutritional Breakdown (Estimated per serving): Calories: 200 kcal, Fat: 22 g, Protein: 2 g, Carbs: 1 g Yield: 4 servings

Ingredients:
- 1/2 cup butter
- 1/4 cup heavy cream
- 3 garlic cloves, minced
- Pinch of salt
- Optional: 1 tsp lemon juice or fresh herbs (like thyme or rosemary)

Instructions:
1. Melt Butter: In a small saucepan over medium heat, melt the butter.
2. Add Garlic: Add the minced garlic and cook for 2-3 minutes until fragrant and lightly golden.
3. Stir in Cream: Lower the heat and slowly stir in the heavy cream, letting it simmer for about 5 minutes until the sauce thickens slightly.
4. Season and Serve: Add a pinch of salt and optional lemon juice or herbs for added flavor. Serve over steaks, chicken, or seafood.

CHAPTER 9 DESSERTS

CARNIVORE CHOCOLATE-FREE FUDGE

Prep Time: 5 minutes | **Chill Time:** 2 hours | **Total Time:** 2 hours 5 minutes
Nutritional Breakdown (Estimated per serving): Calories: 300 kcal, Fat: 28 g, Protein: 5 g, Carbs: 1 g Yield: 8 servings

Ingredients:
- 1/2 cup butter, melted
- 1/4 cup beef tallow (or coconut oil for a creamier texture)
- 1/4 cup heavy cream
- 1 tsp vanilla extract (optional)
- 1 tsp ground cinnamon (optional)
- Pinch of salt

Instructions:
1. Mix Ingredients: In a medium bowl, whisk together the melted butter, beef tallow (or coconut oil), heavy cream, vanilla extract, cinnamon (if using), and salt until the mixture is smooth and well combined.
2. Pour into Mold: Line a small dish or silicone mold with parchment paper. Pour the mixture into the mold and smooth the top with a spatula.
3. Chill: Place the dish in the refrigerator for at least 2 hours to allow the fudge to set completely.
4. Slice and Serve: Once the fudge is firm, remove it from the mold and slice into bite-sized squares. Serve cold and enjoy the rich, buttery, melt-in-your-mouth flavor.

CARNIVORE CUSTARD

Prep Time: 5 minutes | **Cook Time:** 25 minutes | **Total Time:** 30 minutes
Nutritional Breakdown: Calories: 300 kcal, Fat: 25 g, Protein: 10 g, Carbs: 1 g Yield: 4 servings

Ingredients:
- 6 egg yolks
- 1 cup heavy cream
- 1 tsp vanilla extract (optional)
- 2 tbsp butter (for greasing)

Instructions:
1. Preheat Oven: Preheat your oven to 325°F. Grease 4 ramekins with butter.
2. Mix Custard: In a bowl, whisk together egg yolks and heavy cream until smooth and fully combined. Add vanilla extract if desired for extra flavor.
3. Prepare Baking Dish: Place the ramekins in a deep baking dish. Pour the custard mixture evenly into the ramekins.
4. Water Bath: Fill the baking dish with hot water until it reaches halfway up the sides of the ramekins.
5. Bake: Place the dish in the oven and bake for 20-25 minutes, or until the custard is just set but slightly jiggly in the center.
6. Cool and Serve: Remove from the oven and allow to cool slightly. Chill in the fridge if desired for a firmer texture before serving.

CHEESE FAT BOMBS

Prep Time: 5 minutes | **Chill Time:** 1 hour | **Total Time:** 1 hour 5 minutes
Nutritional Breakdown (Estimated per serving): Calories: 150 kcal, Fat: 14 g, Protein: 5 g, Carbs: 1 g Yield: 8 small balls

Ingredients:
- 1/2 cup cream cheese, softened
- 2 tbsp butter, softened
- 1 tsp vanilla extract (optional)

Instructions:
1. **Mix Ingredients:** In a bowl, mix the softened cream cheese, butter, and vanilla extract (if using) until smooth and creamy.
2. **Shape Fat Bombs:** Form the mixture into small balls using your hands or a spoon.
3. **Chill:** Place the balls on a parchment-lined tray and refrigerate for at least 1 hour, or until firm.
4. **Serve:** Once firm, enjoy these rich and creamy cheese fat bombs. Store any leftovers in the fridge.

HEAVY CREAM PANNA COTTA

Prep Time: 5 minutes | **Chill Time:** 2 hours | **Total Time:** 2 hours 5 minutes
Nutritional Breakdown: Calories: 250 kcal, Fat: 24 g, Protein: 3 g, Carbs: 1 g Yield: 4 servings

Ingredients:
- 1 cup heavy cream
- 1 tsp gelatin
- 1 tsp vanilla extract (optional)

Instructions:
1. **Heat Cream:** In a small saucepan, gently heat the heavy cream over medium heat until warm, but not boiling.
2. **Dissolve Gelatin:** Stir in the gelatin and whisk until fully dissolved.
3. **Flavor with Vanilla:** Add the vanilla extract (optional) and mix well.
4. **Pour into Ramekins:** Pour the mixture evenly into 4 small ramekins or cups.
5. **Chill:** Place the ramekins in the refrigerator for at least 2 hours, or until fully set and firm.
6. **Serve:** Once chilled, enjoy the panna cotta as a rich and creamy dessert. You can serve it directly from the ramekins or unmold it for a more elegant presentation.

CARNIVORE CHEESECAKE BITES

Prep Time: 10 minutes | **Cook Time:** 20 minutes | **Total Time:** 30 minutes
Nutritional Breakdown (Estimated per serving): Calories: 350 kcal, Fat: 30 g, Protein: 10 g, Carbs: 1 g Yield: 6 cheesecake bites

Ingredients:
- 8 oz cream cheese, softened
- 1/4 cup heavy cream
- 1 egg yolk

Instructions:
1. Preheat Oven: Preheat your oven to 325°F. Line a muffin tin with liners or grease well.
2. Mix Ingredients: In a bowl, mix the softened cream cheese, heavy cream, and egg yolk until the mixture is smooth and creamy.
3. Fill Muffin Tin: Spoon the mixture into the muffin tin, filling each cup about halfway.
4. Bake: Bake for 18-20 minutes, or until the tops are set and lightly golden.
5. Cool and Serve: Allow the cheesecake bites to cool slightly before refrigerating. Enjoy them chilled for a rich, indulgent treat.

VANILLA BUTTER ICE CREAM

Prep Time: 5 minutes | **Chill Time:** 2-3 hours | **Total Time:** 2-3 hours 5 minutes
Nutritional Breakdown: Calories: 250 kcal, Fat: 22 g, Protein: 4 g, Carbs: 1 g Yield: 4 servings

Ingredients:
- 1/2 cup heavy cream
- 2 tbsp butter, melted
- 1 tsp vanilla extract (optional)

Instructions:
1. Mix Ingredients: In a bowl, whisk together the heavy cream, melted butter, and vanilla extract until smooth.
2. Pour into Dish: Pour the mixture into a shallow dish or ice cream maker.
3. Freeze: If using an ice cream maker, follow the manufacturer's instructions. For freezer method, place the dish in the freezer for about 2-3 hours. Stir the mixture every 30 minutes to break up ice crystals and achieve a smooth texture.
4. Serve: Once the ice cream has firmed up to a creamy consistency (after 2-3 hours), scoop and serve.
This gives the ice cream enough time to set properly while being stirred for a smooth, creamy texture.

90-DAY MEAL PLAN

WEEK 1

Day 1
Breakfast: Ham and Mozzarella Breakfast Roll-Ups
Lunch: Crispy Duck Breast
Dinner: Grilled Swordfish with Herb Butter
Snack: Cheddar Cheese Chips

Day 2
Breakfast: Carnivore Breakfast Pizza
Lunch: Smoked Salmon and Cream Cheese Roll-Ups
Dinner: Venison Steak with Mushroom Sauce
Snack: Deviled Eggs

Day 3
Breakfast: Pork Sausage and Cream Cheese Omelette
Lunch: Pork Loin with Parmesan Crust
Dinner: Seared Halibut with Caper Butter Sauce
Snack: Bacon-Wrapped Avocado Bites

Day 4
Breakfast: Bacon & Ground Pork Scramble
Lunch: Grilled Lamb Chops with Garlic Butter
Dinner: Duck Breast and Beef Broth Soup
Snack: Pepperoni Chips

Day 5
Breakfast: Veal Sweetbreads with Garlic Butter
Lunch: Bison Steaks with Bone Broth Reduction
Dinner: Pan-Seared Rabbit with Thyme and Garlic
Snack: Carnivore Meat Chips

Day 6
Breakfast: Baked Eggs with Ricotta and Bacon
Lunch: Carnivore Shepherd's Pie
Dinner: Grilled Octopus with Olive Oil
Snack: Pork Cracklings

Day 7
Breakfast: Smoked Pork Shoulder & Collagen Pancakes
Lunch: Lamb Meatballs with Bone Broth Gravy
Dinner: Lobster and Shrimp Stew
Snack: Duck Fat Crisps

WEEK 2

Day 8
Breakfast: Steak & Eggs
Lunch: Seared Venison Steaks with Herb Reduction
Dinner: Grilled Pork Ribs with Bone Broth Glaze
Snack: Bacon-Wrapped Scallops

Day 9
Breakfast: Ground Beef & Cheese Scramble
Lunch: Pork Rind Crusted Chicken Thighs
Dinner: Carnivore Seafood Soup
Snack: Turkey Bacon Bites

Day 10
Breakfast: Baked Egg and Gouda Cups
Lunch: Beef Kidney and Bacon Stir-Fry
Dinner: Grilled Prawns with Garlic and Lemon
Snack: Pork Rind Nachos

Day 11
Breakfast: Sausage & Egg Scramble
Lunch: Smoked Salmon and Cream Cheese Roll-Ups
Dinner: Baked Beef Short Ribs with Tallow
Snack: Cheddar Cheese Chips

Day 12
Breakfast: Bacon & Egg Skillet
Lunch: Grilled Beef Tongue with Mustard Sauce
Dinner: Grilled Sardines with Garlic and Herb Butter
Snack: Pepperoni Chips

Day 13
Breakfast: Crispy Pork Belly Bites
Lunch: Pan-Seared Ribeye with Compound Butter
Dinner: Pork Belly Skewers
Snack: Deviled Eggs

Day 14
Breakfast: Carnivore Omelette
Lunch: Pork Chops with Crispy Skin
Dinner: Seared Tuna with Avocado
Snack: Bacon-Wrapped Scallops

WEEK 3

Day 15
Breakfast: Baked Eggs with Ricotta and Bacon
Lunch: Carnivore Shepherd's Pie
Dinner: Pan-Fried Salmon with Dill
Snack: Duck Fat Crisps

Day 16
Breakfast: Ham and Mozzarella Breakfast Roll-Ups
Lunch: Bison Steaks with Bone Broth Reduction
Dinner: Pork Tenderloin with Ghee
Snack: Carnivore Meat Chips

Day 17
Breakfast: Smoked Pork Shoulder & Collagen Pancakes
Lunch: Lamb Meatballs with Bone Broth Gravy
Dinner: Seared Halibut with Caper Butter Sauce
Snack: Bacon-Wrapped Avocado Bites

Day 18
Breakfast: Steak & Eggs
Lunch: Pork Loin with Parmesan Crust
Dinner: Grilled Octopus with Olive Oil
Snack: Deviled Eggs

Day 19
Breakfast: Carnivore Breakfast Pizza
Lunch: Smoked Salmon and Cream Cheese Roll-Ups
Dinner: Grilled Shrimp with Lemon Butter
Snack: Pepperoni Chips

Day 20
Breakfast: Pork Sausage and Cream Cheese Omelette
Lunch: Beef Kidney and Bacon Stir-Fry
Dinner: Duck Breast and Beef Broth Soup
Snack: Cheddar Cheese Chips

Day 21
Breakfast: Ground Beef & Cheese Scramble
Lunch: Grilled Beef Tongue with Mustard Sauce
Dinner: Lobster and Shrimp Stew
Snack: Pork Cracklings

WEEK 4

Day 22
Breakfast: Sausage & Egg Scramble
Lunch: Pan-Seared Ribeye with Compound Butter
Dinner: Venison Steak with Mushroom Sauce
Snack: Bacon-Wrapped Scallops

Day 23
Breakfast: Bacon & Egg Skillet
Lunch: Pork Chops with Crispy Skin
Dinner: Seared Tuna with Avocado
Snack: Turkey Bacon Bites

Day 24
Breakfast: Baked Egg and Gouda Cups
Lunch: Lamb Meatballs with Bone Broth Gravy
Dinner: Grilled Sardines with Garlic and Herb Butter
Snack: Deviled Eggs

Day 25
Breakfast: Crispy Pork Belly Bites
Lunch: Beef Kidney and Bacon Stir-Fry
Dinner: Baked Cod with Olive Oil and Herbs
Snack: Carnivore Meat Chips

Day 26
Breakfast: Veal Sweetbreads with Garlic Butter
Lunch: Bison Steaks with Bone Broth Reduction
Dinner: Seared Halibut with Caper Butter Sauce
Snack: Duck Fat Crisps

Day 27
Breakfast: Carnivore Omelette
Lunch: Pork Loin with Parmesan Crust
Dinner: Grilled Octopus with Olive Oil
Snack: Bacon-Wrapped Avocado Bites

Day 28
Breakfast: Ground Beef & Cheese Scramble
Lunch: Pork Rind Crusted Chicken Thighs
Dinner: Pan-Fried Salmon with Dill
Snack: Pork Rind Nachos

WEEK 5

Day 29
Breakfast: Sausage & Egg Scramble
Lunch: Beef and Ricotta Stuffed Meatballs
Dinner: Seared Tuna with Avocado
Snack: Bacon-Wrapped Avocado Bites

Day 30
Breakfast: Crispy Pork Belly Bites
Lunch: Grilled Beef Tongue with Mustard Sauce
Dinner: Pan-Seared Sole with Sage Butter
Snack: Deviled Eggs

Day 31
Breakfast: Steak & Eggs
Lunch: Lamb Meatballs with Bone Broth Gravy
Dinner: Pork Tenderloin with Ghee
Snack: Cheddar Cheese Chips

Day 32
Breakfast: Baked Egg and Gouda Cups
Lunch: Pork Loin with Parmesan Crust
Dinner: Grilled Shrimp with Lemon Butter
Snack: Duck Fat Crisps

Day 33
Breakfast: Bacon & Egg Skillet
Lunch: Bison Steaks with Bone Broth Reduction
Dinner: Seared Halibut with Caper Butter Sauce
Snack: Turkey Bacon Bites

Day 34
Breakfast: Carnivore Breakfast Pizza
Lunch: Pan-Seared Ribeye with Compound Butter
Dinner: Venison Steak with Mushroom Sauce
Snack: Bacon-Wrapped Scallops

Day 35
Breakfast: Veal Sweetbreads with Garlic Butter
Lunch: Pork Rind Crusted Chicken Thighs
Dinner: Pan-Fried Salmon with Dill
Snack: Pork Cracklings

WEEK 6

Day 36
Breakfast: Ground Beef & Cheese Scramble
Lunch: Beef Kidney and Bacon Stir-Fry
Dinner: Seared Halibut with Caper Butter Sauce
Snack: Cheddar Cheese Chips

Day 37
Breakfast: Sausage & Egg Scramble
Lunch: Smoked Salmon and Cream Cheese Roll-Ups
Dinner: Lobster and Shrimp Stew
Snack: Deviled Eggs

Day 38
Breakfast: Bacon & Egg Skillet
Lunch: Pork Loin with Parmesan Crust
Dinner: Grilled Sardines with Garlic and Herb Butter
Snack: Pepperoni Chips

Day 39
Breakfast: Crispy Pork Belly Bites
Lunch: Grilled Lamb Chops with Garlic Butter
Dinner: Grilled Shrimp with Lemon Butter
Snack: Carnivore Meat Chips

Day 40
Breakfast: Carnivore Breakfast Pizza
Lunch: Lamb Meatballs with Bone Broth Gravy
Dinner: Duck Breast and Beef Broth Soup
Snack: Pork Rind Nachos

Day 41
Breakfast: Pork Sausage and Cream Cheese Omelette
Lunch: Pan-Seared Ribeye with Compound Butter
Dinner: Seared Tuna with Avocado
Snack: Bacon-Wrapped Avocado Bites

Day 42
Breakfast: Ground Beef & Cheese Scramble
Lunch: Bison Steaks with Bone Broth Reduction
Dinner: Pan-Seared Rabbit with Thyme and Garlic
Snack: Deviled Eggs

WEEK 7

Day 43
Breakfast: Baked Egg and Gouda Cups
Lunch: Grilled Lamb Chops with Garlic Butter
Dinner: Grilled Pork Ribs with Bone Broth Glaze
Snack: Duck Fat Crisps

Day 44
Breakfast: Sausage & Egg Scramble
Lunch: Bison Steaks with Bone Broth Reduction
Dinner: Seared Venison Steaks with Herb Reduction
Snack: Bacon-Wrapped Scallops

Day 45
Breakfast: Ham and Mozzarella Breakfast Roll-Ups
Lunch: Beef Kidney and Bacon Stir-Fry
Dinner: Pan-Seared Sole with Sage Butter
Snack: Pork Rind Nachos

Day 46
Breakfast: Veal Sweetbreads with Garlic Butter
Lunch: Beef and Ricotta Stuffed Meatballs
Dinner: Grilled Swordfish with Herb Butter
Snack: Deviled Eggs

Day 47
Breakfast: Carnivore Omelette
Lunch: Pan-Seared Ribeye with Compound Butter
Dinner: Lobster and Shrimp Stew
Snack: Pepperoni Chips

Day 48
Breakfast: Ground Beef & Cheese Scramble
Lunch: Pork Loin with Parmesan Crust
Dinner: Baked Cod with Olive Oil and Herbs
Snack: Carnivore Meat Chips

Day 49
Breakfast: Steak & Eggs
Lunch: Grilled Beef Tongue with Mustard Sauce
Dinner: Pan-Seared Rabbit with Thyme and Garlic
Snack: Turkey Bacon Bites

WEEK 8

Day 50
Breakfast: Bacon & Ground Pork Scramble
Lunch: Crispy Duck Breast
Dinner: Pan-Fried Salmon with Dill
Snack: Bacon-Wrapped Avocado Bites

Day 51
Breakfast: Carnivore Breakfast Pizza
Lunch: Smoked Salmon and Cream Cheese Roll-Ups
Dinner: Seared Halibut with Caper Butter Sauce
Snack: Pork Cracklings

Day 52
Breakfast: Smoked Pork Shoulder & Collagen Pancakes
Lunch: Pork Rind Crusted Chicken Thighs
Dinner: Grilled Mackerel with Garlic
Snack: Cheddar Cheese Chips

Day 53
Breakfast: Baked Eggs with Ricotta and Bacon
Lunch: Bison Steaks with Bone Broth Reduction
Dinner: Venison Steak with Mushroom Sauce
Snack: Duck Fat Crisps

Day 54
Breakfast: Veal Sweetbreads with Garlic Butter
Lunch: Grilled Lamb Chops with Garlic Butter
Dinner: Grilled Sardines with Garlic and Herb Butter
Snack: Deviled Eggs

Day 55
Breakfast: Pork Sausage and Cream Cheese Omelette
Lunch: Lamb Meatballs with Bone Broth Gravy
Dinner: Pan-Seared Barramundi with Herb Butter
Snack: Pepperoni Chips

Day 56
Breakfast: Ground Beef & Cheese Scramble
Lunch: Pan-Seared Ribeye with Compound Butter
Dinner: Bison Meatballs with Bone Broth Gravy
Snack: Bacon-Wrapped Scallops

WEEK 9

Day 57
Breakfast: Crispy Pork Belly Bites
Lunch: Pork Chops with Crispy Skin
Dinner: Grilled Octopus with Olive Oil
Snack: Turkey Bacon Bites

Day 58
Breakfast: Steak & Eggs
Lunch: Beef and Ricotta Stuffed Meatballs
Dinner: Grilled Prawns with Garlic and Lemon
Snack: Carnivore Meat Chips

Day 59
Breakfast: Carnivore Omelette
Lunch: Grilled Lamb Chops with Garlic Butter
Dinner: Seared Tuna with Avocado
Snack: Pork Cracklings

Day 60
Breakfast: Ham and Mozzarella Breakfast Roll-Ups
Lunch: Smoked Salmon and Cream Cheese Roll-Ups
Dinner: Baked Beef Short Ribs with Tallow
Snack: Cheddar Cheese Chips

Day 61
Breakfast: Baked Egg and Gouda Cups
Lunch: Grilled Beef Tongue with Mustard Sauce
Dinner: Venison Steak with Mushroom Sauce
Snack: Pepperoni Chips

Day 62
Breakfast: Ground Beef & Cheese Scramble
Lunch: Crispy Duck Breast
Dinner: Lobster and Shrimp Stew
Snack: Duck Fat Crisps

Day 63
Breakfast: Pork Sausage and Cream Cheese Omelette
Lunch: Bison Steaks with Bone Broth Reduction
Dinner: Grilled Swordfish with Herb Butter
Snack: Deviled Eggs

WEEK 10

Day 64
Breakfast: Veal Sweetbreads with Garlic Butter
Lunch: Pork Rind Crusted Chicken Thighs
Dinner: Pan-Seared Rabbit with Thyme and Garlic
Snack: Carnivore Meat Chips

Day 65
Breakfast: Crispy Pork Belly Bites
Lunch: Grilled Lamb Chops with Garlic Butter
Dinner: Seared Halibut with Caper Butter Sauce
Snack: Cheddar Cheese Chips

Day 66
Breakfast: Carnivore Omelette
Lunch: Beef Kidney and Bacon Stir-Fry
Dinner: Baked Cod with Olive Oil and Herbs
Snack: Bacon-Wrapped Scallops

Day 67
Breakfast: Bacon & Ground Pork Scramble
Lunch: Pork Loin with Parmesan Crust
Dinner: Grilled Octopus with Olive Oil
Snack: Pepperoni Chips

Day 68
Breakfast: Steak & Eggs
Lunch: Grilled Beef Tongue with Mustard Sauce
Dinner: Seared Tuna with Avocado
Snack: Pork Rind Nachos

Day 69
Breakfast: Ground Beef & Cheese Scramble
Lunch: Pan-Seared Ribeye with Compound Butter
Dinner: Pan-Fried Salmon with Dill
Snack: Turkey Bacon Bites

Day 70
Breakfast: Baked Eggs with Ricotta and Bacon
Lunch: Lamb Meatballs with Bone Broth Gravy
Dinner: Grilled Prawns with Garlic and Lemon
Snack: Duck Fat Crisps

WEEK 11

Day 71
Breakfast: Carnivore Breakfast Pizza
Lunch: Beef and Ricotta Stuffed Meatballs
Dinner: Bison Meatballs with Bone Broth Gravy
Snack: Bacon-Wrapped Avocado Bites

Day 72
Breakfast: Ham and Mozzarella Breakfast Roll-Ups
Lunch: Smoked Salmon and Cream Cheese Roll-Ups
Dinner: Grilled Sardines with Garlic and Herb Butter
Snack: Deviled Eggs

Day 73
Breakfast: Crispy Pork Belly Bites
Lunch: Bison Steaks with Bone Broth Reduction
Dinner: Grilled Swordfish with Herb Butter
Snack: Carnivore Meat Chips

Day 74
Breakfast: Ground Beef & Cheese Scramble
Lunch: Pork Rind Crusted Chicken Thighs
Dinner: Seared Venison Steaks with Herb Reduction
Snack: Bacon-Wrapped Scallops

Day 75
Breakfast: Bacon & Egg Skillet
Lunch: Pan-Seared Ribeye with Compound Butter
Dinner: Seared Halibut with Caper Butter Sauce
Snack: Turkey Bacon Bites

Day 76
Breakfast: Veal Sweetbreads with Garlic Butter
Lunch: Grilled Beef Tongue with Mustard Sauce
Dinner: Grilled Shrimp with Lemon Butter
Snack: Duck Fat Crisps

Day 77
Breakfast: Baked Egg and Gouda Cups
Lunch: Crispy Duck Breast
Dinner: Pan-Seared Sole with Sage Butter
Snack: Pork Rind Nachos

WEEK 12

Day 78
Breakfast: Sausage & Egg Scramble
Lunch: Beef Kidney and Bacon Stir-Fry
Dinner: Pan-Seared Barramundi with Herb Butter
Snack: Cheddar Cheese Chips

Day 79
Breakfast: Carnivore Omelette
Lunch: Lamb Meatballs with Bone Broth Gravy
Dinner: Grilled Octopus with Olive Oil
Snack: Bacon-Wrapped Avocado Bites

Day 80
Breakfast: Crispy Pork Belly Bites
Lunch: Bison Steaks with Bone Broth Reduction
Dinner: Seared Venison Steaks with Herb Reduction
Snack: Deviled Eggs

Day 81
Breakfast: Ground Beef & Cheese Scramble
Lunch: Pork Loin with Parmesan Crust
Dinner: Grilled Swordfish with Herb Butter
Snack: Pepperoni Chips

Day 82
Breakfast: Steak & Eggs
Lunch: Smoked Salmon and Cream Cheese Roll-Ups
Dinner: Grilled Prawns with Garlic and Lemon
Snack: Pork Cracklings

Day 83
Breakfast: Ham and Mozzarella Breakfast Roll-Ups
Lunch: Pan-Seared Ribeye with Compound Butter
Dinner: Lobster and Shrimp Stew
Snack: Duck Fat Crisps

Day 84
Breakfast: Carnivore Breakfast Pizza
Lunch: Beef and Ricotta Stuffed Meatballs
Dinner: Baked Cod with Olive Oil and Herbs
Snack: Cheddar Cheese Chips

WEEK 13

Day 85
Breakfast: Veal Sweetbreads with Garlic Butter
Lunch: Pork Rind Crusted Chicken Thighs
Dinner: Grilled Sardines with Garlic and Herb Butter
Snack: Carnivore Meat Chips

Day 86
Breakfast: Bacon & Ground Pork Scramble
Lunch: Lamb Meatballs with Bone Broth Gravy
Dinner: Grilled Shrimp with Lemon Butter
Snack: Pepperoni Chips

Day 87
Breakfast: Steak & Eggs
Lunch: Beef Kidney and Bacon Stir-Fry
Dinner: Seared Halibut with Caper Butter Sauce
Snack: Deviled Eggs

Day 88
Breakfast: Ground Beef & Cheese Scramble
Lunch: Crispy Duck Breast
Dinner: Seared Venison Steaks with Herb Reduction
Snack: Duck Fat Crisps

Day 89
Breakfast: Pork Sausage and Cream Cheese Omelette
Lunch: Pan-Seared Ribeye with Compound Butter
Dinner: Pan-Seared Rabbit with Thyme and Garlic
Snack: Bacon-Wrapped Scallops

Day 90
Breakfast: Carnivore Omelette
Lunch: Bison Steaks with Bone Broth Reduction
Dinner: Grilled Octopus with Olive Oil
Snack: Turkey Bacon Bites

SHOPPING LIST

WEEK 1

Meat & Seafood:
Ham: 4 slices
Duck breast: 2 breasts (skin-on)
Swordfish: 2 steaks
Smoked salmon: 4 oz
Venison steak: 2 steaks
Pork sausage: 1/2 lb
Pork loin: 1 lb
Halibut: 2 fillets
Bacon: 14 slices (6 for Day 4, 8 for snacks)
Ground pork: 1 lb
Lamb chops: 4 chops
Bison steaks: 2
Rabbit: 1 whole (cut into pieces)
Veal sweetbreads: 1 lb
Pork shoulder (smoked): 1 lb (shredded)
Ground lamb: 1 lb
Lobster tail: 1
Shrimp: 1/2 lb (peeled and deveined)
Octopus: 1/2 lb
Ground beef: 1 lb
Bone broth: 1 cup (for sauces and soups)

Dairy:
Mozzarella cheese (shredded): 1/4 cup
Cheddar cheese (shredded): 1 cup
Cream cheese: 6 oz
Ricotta cheese: 1/4 cup

Eggs:
Large eggs: 30 eggs

Fats, Oils & Butters:
Butter: 10 tbsp (for various cooking needs)
Beef tallow: 2 tbsp
Duck fat: 2 tbsp
Olive oil: 6 tbsp

Vegetables & Herbs:
Garlic cloves: 4 (minced)
Fresh thyme: 1 tsp (chopped)
Fresh herbs (thyme or rosemary): 1 tsp
Parsley (fresh): 1 tbsp (chopped)
Capers: 1 tbsp
Mushrooms (sliced): 1 cup
Avocados: 2 (for bacon-wrapped avocado bites)

Other:
Pork rinds: 1/2 lb (for snacks)
Crushed pork rinds: 1/2 cup (for Shepherd's Pie and Meatballs)
Collagen powder: 1/2 cup (for pancakes)
Pepperoni slices: 1 cup
Salt and pepper to taste (for seasoning)

WEEK 2

Meat & Seafood:
Ribeye steaks: 2
Venison steaks: 2
Pork ribs: 2 lbs
Scallops: 24 large
Ground beef: 1 lb
Pork thighs (skin-on): 4
Beef kidney: 1/2 lb
Bacon: 12 slices (6 for Day 12, 6 for snacks)
Pork sausage: 4 sausages
Smoked salmon: 4 oz
Beef short ribs: 2 lbs
Beef tongue: 1 lb
Sardines: 6 whole (cleaned)
Pork belly: 1 lb
Pork chops: 2 bone-in, skin-on
Tuna steaks: 2
Turkey bacon: 8 slices
Prawns: 1 lb (peeled and deveined)
Bone broth: 1 cup (for soups and sauces)

Dairy:
Gouda cheese (shredded): 1/4 cup
Cheddar cheese (shredded): 1/2 cup
Cream cheese: 2 oz

Eggs:
Large eggs: 22 eggs

Fats, Oils & Butters:
Butter: 12 tbsp (for various cooking needs)
Beef tallow: 6 tbsp
Olive oil: 4 tbsp

Vegetables & Herbs:
Garlic cloves: 6 (minced)
Fresh thyme: 1 tsp (chopped)
Fresh parsley: 1 tbsp (chopped)
Capers: 1 tbsp
Avocados: 1 (for seared tuna with avocado)

Other:
Pork rinds: 2 cups (for crusting and snacks)
Pepperoni slices: 1 cup
Salt and pepper to taste (for seasoning)

WEEK 3

Meat & Seafood:
Bacon: 14 slices (for various meals and snacks)
Ground beef: 2 lbs
Bison steaks: 2
Pork tenderloin: 1 lb
Smoked pork shoulder: 1 lb (shredded)
Lamb: 1 lb (for meatballs)
Halibut fillets: 2
Ribeye steak: 2 steaks
Pork loin: 1 lb
Octopus: 1/2 lb
Shrimp: 1 lb (peeled and deveined)
Smoked salmon: 4 oz
Pork sausage: 1/2 lb
Beef kidney: 1/2 lb
Duck breast: 2 breasts (skin-on)
Beef tongue: 1 lb
Lobster tail: 1 tail
Shrimp: 1/2 lb (for lobster and shrimp stew)
Ground lamb: 1 lb (for Shepherd's Pie)
Salmon fillets: 2
Pork loin: 1 lb
Avocados: 2 (for bacon-wrapped bites)
Bone broth: 2 cups (for sauces and soups)

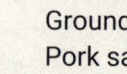

Dairy:
Mozzarella cheese (shredded): 1/4 cup
Cheddar cheese (shredded): 1 cup
Cream cheese: 4 oz
Ricotta cheese: 1/4 cup
Parmesan cheese: 1/4 cup

Eggs:
Large eggs: 32 eggs

Fats, Oils & Butters:
Butter: 14 tbsp (for various meals)
Ghee: 2 tbsp
Duck fat: 2 tbsp
Olive oil: 4 tbsp

Vegetables & Herbs:
Garlic cloves: 4 (minced)
Fresh thyme: 1 tsp (chopped)
Fresh dill: 1 tsp
Fresh parsley: 1 tbsp (chopped)
Capers: 1 tbsp
Lemon juice: 1 tsp

Other:
Pork rinds: 2 cups (for crusting and snacks)
Collagen powder: 1/2 cup (for pancakes)
Pepperoni slices: 1 cup
Salt and pepper to taste (for seasoning)

WEEK 4

Meat & Seafood:
Ground beef: 2 lbs
Pork sausage: 4 sausages
Ribeye steaks: 2
Venison steaks: 2
Scallops: 12 large
Bacon: 16 slices (for various meals and snacks)
Pork chops (bone-in, skin-on): 2
Tuna steaks: 2
Turkey bacon: 8 slices
Lamb: 1 lb (for meatballs)
Sardines: 6 whole (cleaned)
Pork belly: 1 lb
Beef kidney: 1/2 lb
Cod fillets: 2
Veal sweetbreads: 1 lb
Bison steaks: 2
Halibut fillets: 2
Pork loin: 1 lb
Octopus: 1/2 lb
Salmon fillets: 2
Chicken thighs (skin-on): 4 thighs
Avocados: 2 (for bacon-wrapped bites)
Bone broth: 1 cup (for sauces and soups)

Dairy:
Gouda cheese (shredded): 1/4 cup
Cheddar cheese (shredded): 1 cup
Parmesan cheese: 1/4 cup
Cream cheese: 2 oz

Eggs:
Large eggs: 26 eggs

Fats, Oils & Butters:
Butter: 12 tbsp (for various meals)
Beef tallow: 4 tbsp
Olive oil: 6 tbsp
Duck fat: 2 tbsp

Vegetables & Herbs:
Garlic cloves: 6 (minced)
Fresh thyme: 1 tsp (chopped)
Fresh parsley: 1 tbsp (chopped)
Fresh dill: 1 tsp
Capers: 1 tbsp
Lemon juice: 1 tsp

Other:
Pork rinds: 2 cups (for crusting and snacks)
Pepperoni slices: 1 cup
Salt and pepper to taste (for seasoning)

WEEK 5

Meat & Seafood:
Ground beef: 2 lbs
Pork sausage: 4 sausages
Ribeye steaks: 2
Venison steaks: 2
Scallops: 12 large
Bacon: 16 slices (for various meals and snacks)
Pork chops (bone-in, skin-on): 2
Tuna steaks: 2
Turkey bacon: 8 slices
Lamb: 1 lb (for meatballs)
Sardines: 6 whole (cleaned)
Pork belly: 1 lb
Beef kidney: 1/2 lb
Cod fillets: 2
Veal sweetbreads: 1 lb
Bison steaks: 2
Halibut fillets: 2
Pork loin: 1 lb
Octopus: 1/2 lb
Salmon fillets: 2
Chicken thighs (skin-on): 4 thighs
Avocados: 2 (for bacon-wrapped bites)
Bone broth: 1 cup (for sauces and soups)

Dairy:
Gouda cheese (shredded): 1/4 cup
Cheddar cheese (shredded): 1 cup
Parmesan cheese: 1/4 cup
Cream cheese: 2 oz

Eggs:
Large eggs: 26 eggs

Fats, Oils & Butters:
Butter: 12 tbsp (for various meals)
Beef tallow: 4 tbsp
Olive oil: 6 tbsp
Duck fat: 2 tbsp

Vegetables & Herbs:
Garlic cloves: 6 (minced)
Fresh thyme: 1 tsp (chopped)
Fresh parsley: 1 tbsp (chopped)
Fresh dill: 1 tsp
Capers: 1 tbsp
Lemon juice: 1 tsp

Other:
Pork rinds: 2 cups (for crusting and snacks)
Pepperoni slices: 1 cup
Salt and pepper to taste (for seasoning)

WEEK 6

Meat & Seafood:
Ground beef: 2 lbs
Pork sausage: 6 sausages
Bacon: 16 slices (for various meals and snacks)
Beef kidney: 1/2 lb
Halibut fillets: 2
Smoked salmon: 4 oz
Shrimp: 1 lb (peeled and deveined)
Lobster tail: 1
Pork loin: 1 lb
Sardines: 6 whole (cleaned)
Pork belly: 1 lb
Lamb chops: 4 chops
Lamb (ground, for meatballs): 1 lb
Duck breast: 2 breasts (skin-on)
Ribeye steaks: 2
Tuna steaks: 2
Bison steaks: 2
Rabbit: 1 whole (cut into pieces)
Avocados: 2 (for bacon-wrapped bites)
Bone broth: 2 cups (for sauces and soups)

Dairy:
Cheddar cheese (shredded): 1 cup
Cream cheese: 6 oz
Parmesan cheese: 1/4 cup

Eggs:
Large eggs: 32 eggs

Fats, Oils & Butters:
Butter: 12 tbsp (for various meals)
Beef tallow: 4 tbsp
Olive oil: 4 tbsp

Vegetables & Herbs:
Garlic cloves: 6 (minced)
Fresh thyme: 1 tsp (chopped)
Fresh parsley: 1 tbsp (chopped)
Capers: 1 tbsp
Lemon juice: 1 tsp

Other:
Pork rinds: 2 cups (for crusting and snacks)
Pepperoni slices: 1 cup
Salt and pepper to taste (for seasoning)

WEEK 7

Meat & Seafood:
Ground beef: 1 lb
Pork sausage: 4 sausages
Bacon: 12 slices (for various meals and snacks)
Lamb chops: 4 chops
Pork ribs: 2 lbs
Bison steaks: 2
Venison steaks: 2

Ham: 4 slices
Beef kidney: 1/2 lb
Sole fillets: 2
Veal sweetbreads: 1 lb
Ground beef: 1 lb (for stuffed meatballs)
Swordfish steaks: 2
Ribeye steaks: 2
Lobster tail: 1
Shrimp: 1 lb (peeled and deveined)
Pork loin: 1 lb
Cod fillets: 2
Beef tongue: 1 lb
Rabbit: 1 whole (cut into pieces)
Turkey bacon: 8 slices
Avocados: 2 (for bacon-wrapped bites)
Bone broth: 1 cup (for sauces and soups)

Dairy:
Gouda cheese (shredded): 1/4 cup
Mozzarella cheese (shredded): 1/4 cup
Ricotta cheese: 1/2 cup
Cheddar cheese (shredded): 1 cup

Eggs:
Large eggs: 26 eggs

Fats, Oils & Butters:
Butter: 12 tbsp (for various meals)
Beef tallow: 4 tbsp
Duck fat: 2 tbsp
Olive oil: 4 tbsp

Vegetables & Herbs:
Garlic cloves: 6 (minced)
Fresh thyme: 1 tsp (chopped)
Fresh sage: 1 tsp
Fresh parsley: 1 tbsp (chopped)
Capers: 1 tbsp
Lemon juice: 1 tsp

Other:
Pork rinds: 2 cups (for crusting and snacks)
Pepperoni slices: 1 cup Salt and pepper to taste (for seasoning)

WEEK 8

Meat & Seafood:
Ground beef: 2 lbs
Pork sausage: 4 sausages
Bacon: 14 slices (for various meals and snacks)
Ground pork: 1 lb
Duck breast: 2 breasts (skin-on)
Salmon fillets: 2
Smoked pork shoulder: 1 lb (shredded)
Chicken thighs (skin-on): 4 thighs
Mackerel fillets: 2
Smoked salmon: 4 oz

Halibut fillets: 2
Bison steaks: 2
Venison steaks: 2
Veal sweetbreads: 1 lb
Lamb chops: 4 chops
Sardines: 6 whole (cleaned)
Barramundi fillets: 2
Lamb (for meatballs): 1 lb
Bison (ground, for meatballs): 1 lb
Scallops: 12 large
Avocados: 2 (for bacon-wrapped bites)
Bone broth: 2 cups (for sauces and soups)

Dairy:
Ricotta cheese: 1/4 cup
Cheddar cheese (shredded): 1 cup
Cream cheese: 6 oz

Eggs:
Large eggs: 28 eggs

Fats, Oils & Butters:
Butter: 12 tbsp (for various meals)
Beef tallow: 4 tbsp
Duck fat: 2 tbsp
Olive oil: 4 tbsp

Vegetables & Herbs:
Garlic cloves: 8 (minced)
Fresh dill: 1 tsp
Fresh parsley: 1 tbsp (chopped)
Capers: 1 tbsp
Lemon juice: 1 tsp

Other:
Pork rinds: 2 cups (for crusting and snacks)
Collagen powder: 1/2 cup (for pancakes)
Pepperoni slices: 1 cup
Salt and pepper to taste (for seasoning)

WEEK 9

Meat & Seafood:
Pork belly: 1 lb
Pork chops: 2 bone-in, skin-on
Octopus: 1/2 lb
Turkey bacon: 8 slices
Ribeye steak: 2 steaks
Ground beef: 1 lb
Ground pork (for stuffed meatballs): 1 lb
Prawns: 1 lb (peeled and deveined)
Lamb chops: 4 chops
Tuna steaks: 2
Ham: 4 slices
Smoked salmon: 4 oz
Beef short ribs: 2 lbs
Beef tongue: 1 lb
Venison steaks: 2

Duck breast: 2 breasts (skin-on)
Lobster tail: 1
Shrimp: 1 lb (peeled and deveined)
Bison steaks: 2
Swordfish steaks: 2
Bone broth: 1 cup (for sauces and soups)
Dairy:
Mozzarella cheese (shredded): 1/4 cup
Gouda cheese (shredded): 1/4 cup
Ricotta cheese: 1/2 cup
Cheddar cheese (shredded): 1 cup
Cream cheese: 4 oz
Eggs:
Large eggs: 26 eggs
Fats, Oils & Butters:
Butter: 10 tbsp (for various meals)
Beef tallow: 4 tbsp
Duck fat: 2 tbsp
Olive oil: 4 tbsp
Vegetables & Herbs:
Garlic cloves: 6 (minced)
Fresh thyme: 1 tsp
Fresh parsley: 1 tbsp (chopped)
Capers: 1 tbsp
Lemon juice: 1 tsp
Other:
Pork rinds: 2 cups (for crusting and snacks)
Pepperoni slices: 1 cup
Salt and pepper to taste (for seasoning)

WEEK 10

Meat & Seafood:
Veal sweetbreads: 1 lb
Pork belly: 1 lb
Pork thighs (skin-on, for crusting): 4 thighs
Rabbit: 1 whole (cut into pieces)
Lamb chops: 4 chops
Halibut fillets: 2
Ground pork: 1 lb
Beef kidney: 1/2 lb
Cod fillets: 2
Bacon: 12 slices (for various meals and snacks)
Pork loin: 1 lb
Octopus: 1/2 lb
Beef tongue: 1 lb
Tuna steaks: 2
Ground beef: 1 lb
Ribeye steaks: 2
Salmon fillets: 2
Prawns: 1 lb (peeled and deveined)

Veal sweetbreads: 1 lb
Pork belly: 1 lb
Pork thighs (skin-on, for crusting): 4 thighs
Rabbit: 1 whole (cut into pieces)
Lamb (for meatballs): 1 lb
Scallops: 12 large
Turkey bacon: 8 slices
Bone broth: 1 cup (for sauces and soups)
Dairy:
Ricotta cheese: 1/4 cup
Cheddar cheese (shredded): 1 cup
Parmesan cheese: 1/4 cup
Cream cheese: 2 oz
Eggs:
Large eggs: 28 eggs
Fats, Oils & Butters:
Butter: 12 tbsp (for various meals)
Beef tallow: 4 tbsp
Duck fat: 2 tbsp
Olive oil: 6 tbsp
Vegetables & Herbs:
Garlic cloves: 6 (minced)
Fresh thyme: 1 tsp (chopped)
Fresh dill: 1 tsp
Fresh parsley: 1 tbsp (chopped)
Capers: 1 tbsp
Lemon juice: 1 tsp
Other:
Pork rinds: 2 cups (for crusting and snacks)
Pepperoni slices: 1 cup
Salt and pepper to taste (for seasoning)

WEEK 11

Meat & Seafood:
Ground beef: 1 lb
Pork belly: 1 lb
Bacon: 12 slices (for various meals and snacks)
Ham: 4 slices
Smoked salmon: 4 oz
Sardines: 6 whole (cleaned)
Bison steaks: 2
Swordfish steaks: 2
Chicken thighs (skin-on, for crusting): 4 thighs
Venison steaks: 2
Ribeye steaks: 2
Halibut fillets: 2
Veal sweetbreads: 1 lb
Beef tongue: 1 lb
Shrimp: 1 lb (peeled and deveined)
Sole fillets: 2
Duck breast: 2 breasts (skin-on)
Ground bison (for meatballs): 1 lb

Ground beef (for meatballs): 1 lb
Scallops: 12 large
Avocados: 2 (for bacon-wrapped bites)
Bone broth: 2 cups (for sauces and soups)

Dairy:
Mozzarella cheese (shredded): 1/4 cup
Gouda cheese (shredded): 1/4 cup
Cheddar cheese (shredded): 1 cup
Ricotta cheese: 1/2 cup
Cream cheese: 4 oz

Eggs:
Large eggs: 28 eggs

Fats, Oils & Butters:
Butter: 12 tbsp (for various meals)
Beef tallow: 4 tbsp
Duck fat: 2 tbsp
Olive oil: 4 tbsp

Vegetables & Herbs:
Garlic cloves: 6 (minced)
Fresh thyme: 1 tsp
Fresh parsley: 1 tbsp (chopped)
Fresh sage: 1 tsp
Capers: 1 tbsp
Lemon juice: 1 tsp

Other:
Pork rinds: 2 cups (for crusting and snacks)
Pepperoni slices: 1 cup
Salt and pepper to taste (for seasoning)

WEEK 12

Meat & Seafood:
Ground beef: 2 lbs
Pork sausage: 4 sausages
Bacon: 12 slices (for various meals and snacks)
Beef kidney: 1/2 lb
Barramundi fillets: 2
Lamb (for meatballs): 1 lb
Octopus: 1/2 lb
Bison steaks: 2
Venison steaks: 2
Pork loin: 1 lb
Swordfish steaks: 2
Smoked salmon: 4 oz
Prawns: 1 lb (peeled and deveined)
Ribeye steaks: 2
Lobster tail: 1
Shrimp: 1 lb (peeled and deveined)
Cod fillets: 2
Avocados: 2 (for bacon-wrapped bites)
Ground beef (for stuffed meatballs): 1 lb
Bone broth: 2 cups (for sauces and soups)

Dairy:
Mozzarella cheese (shredded): 1/4 cup
Cheddar cheese (shredded): 1 1/4 cups
Ricotta cheese: 1/2 cup
Cream cheese: 4 oz
Parmesan cheese: 1/4 cup

Eggs:
Large eggs: 26 eggs

Fats, Oils & Butters:
Butter: 12 tbsp (for various meals)
Beef tallow: 4 tbsp
Duck fat: 2 tbsp
Olive oil: 4 tbsp

Vegetables & Herbs:
Garlic cloves: 6 (minced)
Fresh thyme: 1 tsp
Fresh parsley: 1 tbsp (chopped)
Capers: 1 tbsp
Lemon juice: 1 tsp

Other:
Pork rinds: 2 cups (for crusting and snacks)
Pepperoni slices: 1 cup
Salt and pepper to taste (for seasoning)

WEEK 13

Meat & Seafood: 
Veal sweetbreads: 1 lb
Pork sausage: 4 sausages
Bacon: 14 slices (for various meals and snacks)
Ground pork: 1 lb
Lamb (for meatballs): 1 lb
Shrimp: 1 lb (peeled and deveined)
Beef kidney: 1/2 lb
Halibut fillets: 2
Ground beef: 1 lb
Duck breast: 2 breasts (skin-on)
Venison steaks: 2
Ribeye steaks: 2
Rabbit: 1 whole (cut into pieces)
Scallops: 12 large
Bison steaks: 2
Octopus: 1/2 lb
Sardines: 6 whole (cleaned)
Chicken thighs (skin-on, for crusting): 4 thighs
Avocados: 2 (for bacon-wrapped bites)
Bone broth: 1 cup (for sauces and soups)

Dairy:
Cheddar cheese (shredded): 1 cup
Cream cheese: 4 oz

Eggs:
Large eggs: 26 eggs

Fats, Oils & Butters:
Butter: 10 tbsp (for various meals)
Beef tallow: 4 tbsp
Duck fat: 2 tbsp
Olive oil: 4 tbsp

Vegetables & Herbs:
Garlic cloves: 6 (minced)
Fresh thyme: 1 tsp (chopped)
Fresh parsley: 1 tbsp (chopped)
Capers: 1 tbsp
Lemon juice: 1 tsp

Other:
Pork rinds: 2 cups (for crusting and snacks)
Pepperoni slices: 1 cup
Salt and pepper to taste (for seasoning)

CONCLUSION

Congratulations on reaching the end of the Lazy Carnivore Diet Cookbook! We hope this collection of recipes has shown you just how simple and enjoyable the carnivore lifestyle can be. From rich, succulent meats to fresh, flavorful seafood, these meals were carefully crafted to provide variety, satisfaction, and most importantly, ease. With minimal cleanup and straightforward ingredients, this book was designed to fit seamlessly into your busy life, making healthy eating both achievable and delicious.

Throughout these pages, we've aimed to guide you on a path to better health, offering not just recipes but practical insights from nutritionist Phoebe Buckley. Whether your focus is on weight loss, improving energy, or enhancing mental clarity, we trust you've found valuable tips to support your personal goals. The thoughtfully curated 90-day meal plan has hopefully taken the guesswork out of meal planning, allowing you to focus on enjoying the journey and the benefits that come with it.

As you continue your carnivore journey, remember that it's about progress, not perfection. The recipes and advice in this book are here to inspire and support you, whether you're new to the carnivore diet or have been following it for years. We hope you feel empowered to customize the protein-to-fat ratios and adapt the meals to suit your evolving tastes and needs, all while embracing the simplicity that makes this diet so approachable.

We would love to hear about your experience with the cookbook! If you've enjoyed the recipes or found the book helpful, we'd be truly grateful if you could take a moment to leave an honest review on Amazon. Your feedback not only helps others discover the benefits of the carnivore lifestyle but also enables us to continue improving and creating content that resonates with readers like you. Reviews are an important way for us to understand what works and where we can grow.

Thank you for trusting the Lazy Carnivore Diet Cookbook to guide you on your health journey. We hope these recipes continue to nourish both your body and your love for simple, flavorful food. Here's to many more satisfying meals, newfound energy, and a healthier, happier you!

Made in United States
Cleveland, OH
30 April 2025

16539760R00042